Suzanne Mulholland

The
BATCH
LADY

Meal Planner

HQ

HQ

An imprint of HarperCollinsPublishers Ltd

1 London Bridge Street

London SE1 9GF

10 9 8 7 6 5 4 3 2 1

First published in Great Britain by HQ
An imprint of HarperCollinsPublishers
Ltd 2020

Text Copyright © Suzanne Mulholland
2020

Suzanne Mulholland asserts the moral
right to be identified as the author of
this work. A catalogue record for this
book is available from the British Library.

ISBN 978-0-00-841820-5

Design: Georgie Hewitt
Project Editor: Daniel Hurst

Printed and bound in Italy

Our policy is to use papers that are
natural, renewable and recyclable
products and made from wood grown
in sustainable forests. The logging and
manufacturing processes conform to the
legal environmental regulations of the
country of origin.

For more information visit:
www.harpercollins.co.uk/green

batch-cook meals for the week ahead and what your freezer is already stocked with for tasty dinners in a hurry. (More information on the weekly planner can be found on pp. 7–15.)

After each weekly planner, you will find a handy shopping list to complete for that week's meals. The lists are broken into sections by type of ingredient (fresh fruit and veg, meat, storecupboard, frozen etc.), enabling you to zip round the supermarket without getting distracted by things you don't need, and saving you time and money in the process. (More information on the weekly shopping lists can be found on p.16.)

At the back of the book there are rolling lists that will enable you to see at a glance whicht ingredients you already have in the storecupboard or freezer, and which meals you already have prepped and ready to go. When putting together your weekly meal planners and shopping lists, simply refer back to these to see what you already have to hand. (More information on the storecupboard and freezer lists can be found on p.17.)

Remember that the ultimate aim here is to give yourself the headspace to relax and enjoy the fun stuff, so try not to stress. Once you've got into the flow of planning your meals in this way you will be amazed by how much time and energy you've been able to reclaim.

Believe in the batch!

Suzanne

BATCH COMMANDMENTS

When planning your food for the week, follow these rules and you can't go wrong!

- **Life doesn't always go to plan.** Make a firm meal plan for 3–4 days of the week, then pencil in a rough outline for others. It's a good idea to leave a few nights blank for when plans change, to use up leftovers or just for those days when you fancy getting a takeaway!

- **Think about meals in terms of time** and pair them up with your life plan accordingly. Busy night? Pull a fast, pre-made meal from the freezer. Lazy Sunday? Why not cook a roast?

- **Eat meals from your freezer a few nights per week** so you are not always cooking from scratch.

- **Double up!** Cooking double quantities often takes no extra time and gives you two full meals in the time it would take to make just one. Simply eat one on the day and store the other in the freezer.

- **Allocate a 'fill-your-freezer' hour once a month** when you focus on cooking meals to freeze for later. To save time, make meals that use similar ingredients. (The twinned meals in *The Batch Lady* cookbook are a great starting point.)

- **Get the family involved.** Asking your family what they'd like to eat in the week ahead takes the pressure off you to come up with ideas and helps keep everyone happy!

- **Stick to what you know.** It's fun to try something new, but don't take on too much all at once. Add one new recipe to your repetoire each week to start branching out.

- **Be honest!** This planner is for your eyes only; the more 'real' you are, the better the process will work.

Contents

Recipes

WELCOME!

My name is Suzanne Mulholland, though you may know me better as *The Batch Lady*. As a busy mum with a large extended family, I spent many years devising a way of freeing myself from the kitchen, while still putting healthy, home-cooked meals on the table. Drawing on the organisational skills developed during my career as a time-management consultant for businesses, I came up with a method of cooking multiple meals at once and storing them in the freezer for later, and reclaimed much of my precious time in the process. For over three years now, I have been sharing the tips and tricks behind my batch method online and there has been more of an appetite for them than I ever could have imagined.

Since my first cookbook was released, I have received many messages asking for more information on how I plan what to cook and eat each week. The questions have ranged from 'How do you put together a balanced meal plan?' and 'What's the best way to organise a shopping list?' to 'How do I keep track of what's in the freezer?' This planner is the answer to all these questions and more. It contains all of the guides that I personally use to keep myself on track and will give you an instant overview of what you're doing, cooking and eating in the weeks ahead, so that you can plan your meals around your life and not the other way around!

If you're anything like me, as soon as you get everything that's buzzing around your head down onto a piece of paper, you will instantly feel more in control. Spending 20 minutes at the beginning of each week filling in the weekly planners and shopping lists in this book will free up hours of time that you would otherwise spend agonising over what to cook in the evening or running out to the shops for emergency ingredients. Once your planner is filled in, you will be able to see at a glance which nights are your busiest, when you will have more time to

FILLING IN YOUR WEEKLY PLANNER

Planning what you are going to cook and eat for an entire week can feel daunting at first, but once you get the hang of it you'll never look back. After a few weeks, you'll find that the planners almost fill themselves in! Remember, you don't need to plan every night – in fact, it's best not to, as then you can chop and change your plans without any food wastage. Working in this way, if you no longer have time to cook your favourite beef casserole on Wednesday, you can cook it on Friday instead. Flexibility is key.

Start with what you know

We've all got a repertoire of regular meals that we fall back on time and time again. Usually, it's around 10–15 tried-and-tested family favourites that we know will be received well. I call them my 'go-to meals'. When starting to meal plan, it's a good idea to start with these recipes, especially if you're cooking for children, who can get easily spooked if a whole host of food that they don't recognise starts landing on their plate!

Using the space on the next page, write down a list of the meals that are regular favourites in your house – and remember, this isn't about breaking your back to cook everything from scratch. We all need a night off, so if you order pizza once a week and it's something you all enjoy and look forward to, stick it on the list! When you start planning, don't be afraid to take a look at this list for inspiration. These are family favourites that you already know how to make.

My go-to meals

Now we know what works, let's have a think about what doesn't. What would you like to change about the way you and your family eat? Are you trying to cut down on meat or introduce more veg into your diet? Do you feel stuck in a rut and find you're making the same two or three meals over and over again? Are you fed up with shelling out for expensive ready meals and want to cook more from scratch? What new dishes would you like to try? This is your chance to make any changes you want to the food you put on the table – just write them down here.

What I'd like to change

_____

_____

_____

_____

_____

_____

_____

_____

_____

Get planning

Now it's time to plan your first week! The first thing to do is to fill in the 'doing' sections of the planner on Week 1 (pp.20–23). This will allow you to see immediately which days are likely to be busy so that you can plan your meals accordingly. In my house, there are some evenings where it feels like everyone is going in different directions, so having all this information at hand helps me be realistic about what I can get on the table and see, in an instant, who will be there to eat it!

Now you can see what your week looks like, it's time to plan your meals.

For the first week, it's a good idea to go back to your 'go-to meals' list (p.8) and pick the bulk of your meals from there, perhaps throwing in one new recipe that you want to try. When picking the recipes that I am going to eat over a week, I like to make sure that I've got a balance of different flavours and ingredients. If I'm having chicken fajitas on a Monday, maybe I'll have a veggie stir-fry on the Tuesday, then something fish-based on the Wednesday, and so on.

Fill in the 'eating' section of Week 1 over four nights with meals from your 'go-to meals' list, then add in any nights that you plan to have a takeaway, eat out or, of course, have something from the freezer. If you'd like to try something new this week, add that in next, perhaps on a nice quiet evening when you'll have plenty of time. Now that the bulk of your week is planned, you can pencil in plans for the rest, if you like. I only plan five out of seven nights, but you might wish to plan the whole week. It's completely up to you.

BREAKFASTS & LUNCHES

The main focus of this planner is on evening meals, as these are often the most time-consuming. However, if you want to plan your breakfasts and lunches too, then go for it. In my book, you can never be too organised! Midweek breakfasts in my house tend to be cereal or toast eaten in a hurry, so it can feel like a real treat to plan a special breakfast for a weekend, holiday or celebration.

Fresh or frozen?

In the 'eating' section of the weekly planner you'll see tick boxes labelled 'fresh' and 'frozen'. Once you've been batching for a while, you will have a selection of meals ready to go in the freezer, for days when you don't have the time (or inclination) to cook. Marking which meals are coming from the freezer serves as a visual reminder to get the meal out of the freezer to defrost in the fridge, ideally the night before you want to eat it. As an additional reminder, I like to set an alarm on my phone reminding me to whip the meal out of the freezer.

If you're trying to escape the monotony of cooking from scratch every single night, try to cook 2–3 meals a week from your stock of pre-prepared freezer meals, so on busy nights you can just heat and go. If you're new to batching and don't have any meals prepped in the freezer yet, then now is a great time to start building up a supply. That's where the 'cooking' section of the weekly planner comes in.

Cooking versus eating

If you're a new batcher, you may be wondering why each weekly planner has separate sections for 'cooking' and 'eating'. This is where the magic of batching truly happens and how you can really start to reclaim your precious time. In my week there will often be a few magic hours where the kids are out at their friends' houses, my husband is busy with a project and I have the house to myself. While the temptation might be to put my feet up with a biscuit and a nice cup of tea (which definitely happens sometimes!), I mostly use these times to batch meals for the freezer. Doing this ensures that I always have a tasty supply of simple, nutritious meals that I can defrost or cook from frozen and get onto the table with minimal effort in the evenings. This might sound laborious, but it's actually a huge time saver and my recipes always focus on simplicity, so can be prepped with minimal effort. Why not look for a space in your diary and try prepping something for the freezer this week – the Sticky Asian Chicken Traybake on page 208 of this book can be assembled in moments, so is a great place to start.

BATCH DAYS

Once you've planned a few weeks and are a true batching buff, you may find yourself wanting to plan dedicated batching sessions, where you prepare lots of meals for the freezer in one go. When doing this, I often cook meals that use similar ingredients to make it as efficient a process as possible. In this book you'll find dedicated 'Batch Day' planners spaced every six weeks (the first is on page 68), with dedicated shopping lists and meal planners for these days. For more info on my batching method, including how to make 10 meals in 1 hour, take a look at my cookbook or my online recipes at *thebatchlady.com*.

To freeze & double up

In the 'cooking' section of the weekly planner, you'll see tick boxes labelled 'to freeze' and 'double up'. Making a double portion often takes only a few minutes extra, so is a great way of making your time work for you. Say, for example, you are making Spaghetti Bolognese for your evening meal. Why not double up the recipe and put half in the freezer for later? That way, you have two delicious meals in the time it would take to make one!

If you have never done this before then start off small, choosing just one meal per week to double up. Once it's in the freezer you can add it to the 'eating' plan for the following week, ticking the 'frozen' box as you do so, so you know straightaway that you've got a tasty meal ready to go. I promise, once you've enjoyed a few nights of not having to cook, you will be addicted to doubling up!

It's good to decide which recipes you want to double up when planning your food for the week, so that you can factor double ingredients into your weekly shopping list, and ticking these boxes is a great visual reminder that you're planning to make a big batch of a recipe.

Now that you've learnt the basics of how to fill in your meal planner, turn the page to see an example of how the planner works in action.

How long can I store food in the freezer?

It's important to rotate and refresh the food in your freezer regularly, as frozen food still deteriorates. Referring to the chart below can help with this. I also give ideal maximum freezing times in all of my recipes.

FOOD	TIME IN FREEZER
Avocados	3–6 months
Bananas	2–3 months
Blanched vegetables	1 year
Bread	6 months
Butter	3–4 months
Cakes	6 months
Cooked pasta	2 months
Cooked rice	6–8 months
Egg whites and yolks (not in the shell)	1 year
Frozen fruit	1 year
Fruit	12 months
Full meals	3–6 months
Garlic	12 months
Ginger	6 months
Grated cheese	8 months
Herbs	12 months
Ice cream	4 months
Meat (including poultry)	6 months
Milk	3–6 months
Nuts	2 years
Oily fish	4 months
Pastries	4 months
Raw pastry	10 months
Soups and sauces	3 months
Stocks	6 months
White fish	8 months

Example weekly planner

THURSDAY

Cooking
lasagne ✓✓
chilli ✓✓
○○
○○

Eating
chilli ✓○
○○
○○
○○

Here, you can see that I'm batching a lasagne and a chilli at the same time and doubling up on both recipes. One portion of the chilli will be enjoyed for dinner, the second portion will go in the freezer for another day.

Doing
book club – 7pm

FRIDAY

Cooking
fish pie ✓✓
fish chowder ✓✓
○○
○○

Eating
fish pie ✓○
○○
○○
○○

Doing
pub quiz – 8pm
M & D babysitting

I like to batch similar dishes together, such as the fish pie and chowder here, or the lasagne and chilli, above. This not only saves time, but is also cost-effective as you're using many of the same ingredients in both dishes.

On a busy Saturday where the whole family is out all day and the kids need energy for sport, I might pull a hearty breakfast from the freezer and order a treat takeaway in the evening.

SATURDAY

Cooking

RESTOCK / _IN STOCK_

Eating

FRESH / _FREEZER_

breakfast skillet ✓

takeaway!!

Doing

hockey tournament - ALL DAY!!

SUNDAY

Cooking

DOUBLE / _TO FREEZE_

cheesecake ✓

Eating

FRESH / _FREEZER_

roast lamb ✓

roast potatoes ✓

cheesecake ✓

Doing

family round for Sunday lunch

Sundays mean roasts in our house! In this example I am making fresh roast lamb, but saving time by using pre-cooked roast potatoes from the freezer. I am also making a cheesecake, some of which will be eaten on the day and the rest frozen for later.

45

SHOPPING LISTS

Once you've filled in your weekly planner, it's time to put together your shopping list. I always make a shopping list before going to the supermarket and try not to deviate from it. Doing this means that you are only buying things that you know you need, which reduces food waste and saves you money in the process. I like to organise my shopping lists according to the different sections of the supermarket, which makes it easy to zip round and get everything you need in a flash. It also means that you can avoid the temptations of the biscuit and confectionery aisles, so you may well end up eating a bit healthier, too.

Filling in your shopping list

Make a list of all the ingredients needed to make your planned meals, making sure to factor in scaled-up amounts for recipes that you are planning to double up, then run down the list and cross off anything that you know that you already have at home. The storecupboard and freezer lists at the back of this book will help with this. Now write everything you need to buy this week on the shopping list page that follows your weekly planner, using the subheadings to organise the list into different sections. Once that's done, add anything else that you may need for breakfasts and lunches (or treats!) that you haven't planned, and you're ready to shop.

WRITE A 'RUN OUT' LIST

In my house, we have a pad stuck to the fridge that acts as a rolling shopping list that anyone can jot things onto as they get used up. This is great for when someone uses the last of the butter or the shampoo is running low as, in theory, you should never run out of the essentials. My kids like to try and sneak chocolate and ice cream onto our list, which, funnily enough, doesn't always make it home from the shop! Make sure you add anything from your 'run out' list to this week's shopping list.

FREEZER & STORECUPBOARD LISTS

At the back of this book you will find stock lists for both your freezer and storecupboard. I find that keeping a rolling list of what I have in the freezer and kitchen cupboards a huge help when planning my weekly meals. These lists enable you to see, at a glance, what meals and ingredients you already have to hand, saving you from having to do a stocktake every time you go to the shops.

I've allocated plenty of space to these lists, so whether you're working with a huge chest freezer or a smaller, three-drawer version, you should be able to record everything that you have in stock. The best way to approach these lists is to do a full stocktake when just getting started with this book, then cross things off as they get used up and add them on again as you refill your freezer or cupboards.

The 'What's in the Freezer?' list (pp.234–245) is divided into main meals, side dishes and produce, so you can keep track of your batch-cooked meals as well as your stocks of frozen vegetables. To make sure that you're always refreshing the freezer with fresh meals and using up the old ones, I have included a 'date frozen' column, so that you can always make sure that you're using up the oldest food first. Always clearly label your meals with the date and name of the dish before putting them in the freezer so that you don't end up with any UFOs (Unidentified Frozen Objects!).

The 'What's in the Cupboard?' list (pp.246–255) is divided into sections on grains, rice and pasta; cans and jars; oils, sauces and vinegars; herbs and spices; baking ingredients; and miscellaneous, so it can easily be navigated to see how much rice you have in stock or if you have any dried oregano hiding at the back of the cupboard. As with the freezer list, simply cross things off or adjust the quantities as you use them and you will always have a good idea of what ingredients you have to hand.

Dairy QTY QTY

....

....

....

....

....

Storecupboard QTY QTY

....

....

....

....

....

....

Frozen Goods QTY QTY

....

....

....

....

....

Miscellaneous QTY QTY

....

....

....

LEMON DRIZZLE CAKE

Packed with the zing of lemons and topped with a crunchy sugar crown, Lemon Drizzle Cake is everyone's favourite afternoon treat. With this recipe you can freeze individual slices of the cake and remove them from the freezer as needed, that's if you have any leftover to freeze!

PREP: 10 MINUTES
COOK: 40 MINUTES
MAKES 1 x 900G (2LB) LOAF CAKE

¾ cup (180g) unsalted butter, at room temperature
1⅔ cups (220g) self-raising flour
1 tsp baking powder
3 eggs, beaten
zest and juice of 2 lemons
2 tbsp milk
1½ cups (300g) caster sugar
½ tsp salt

01 Preheat the oven to 180°C/350°F/gas mark 4. Grease a 900g (2lb) loaf tin with butter and line with greaseproof paper.

02 In a large bowl, beat together the butter, flour, baking powder, eggs, lemon zest, milk and 1 cup (200g) of the sugar with an electric whisk or wooden spoon until well combined. Pour the mixture into the prepared loaf tin and level it out with the back of a spoon.

03 Transfer to the oven and bake for 35–40 minutes until golden, well risen and a skewer inserted into the centre of the cake comes out clean.

To see a picture of this recipe, visit **thebatchlady.com/mealplanner**

04 While the cake is in the oven, prepare the drizzle by heating the lemon juice and remaining 100g (½ cup) of sugar over a low heat, stirring continuously, for around 5 minutes, until the sugar has melted.

05 Once cooked, remove the cake from the oven and immediately poke holes all over the top with a skewer. Spoon half of the drizzle mixture over the cake, allowing it to soak into the sponge, then spoon over the remaining drizzle.

06 Set the cake aside to cool completely in the tin.

TO SERVE NOW: Once cooled, turn the cake out of the tin, cut into slices and serve.

....

TO FREEZE: Once cooled, turn the cake out of the tin, cut into slices and wrap each in a layer of clingfilm followed by a layer of foil. Store the slices flat in the freezer for up to 3 months.

....

TO SERVE FROM FROZEN: Remove individual slices of the cake from the freezer as needed and set on the counter to defrost. They should be ready to eat in around 30 minutes.

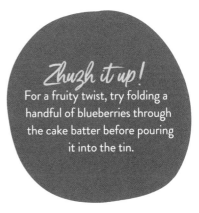

Zhuzh it up!
For a fruity twist, try folding a handful of blueberries through the cake batter before pouring it into the tin.

Batch Day

DATE

_____

Use this page to plan for the days when you want to tackle a dedicated batching session, making several meals at once to fill your freezer. Write a list of the meals that you want to make below, making sure to mark if you're planning to double up any of the recipes. Once you've planned what you're going to cook, use the shopping list opposite to write down what you need to buy. I like to do a special visit to the shops or order online when I'm planning a batch day, as that way I can lay everything out on the sides when I get home and am ready to start, without having to scrabble around in the cupboards trying to find things while I'm cooking.

What I'm cooking

Double Up

○
○
○
○
○
○
○
○
○

Notes

BATCH DAY SHOPPING LIST

Fruit & Vegetables QTY QTY

....

....

....

....

Meat & Fish QTY QTY

....

....

....

....

Dairy QTY QTY

....

....

....

....

Storecupboard QTY QTY

....

....

....

Frozen Goods QTY QTY

....

....

....

WEEK 7

Notes

MONDAY

Cooking

	DOUBLE UP TO FREEZE
	⭘⭘
	⭘⭘
	⭘⭘
	⭘⭘

Eating

	FROZEN FRESH
	⭘⭘
	⭘⭘
	⭘⭘
	⭘⭘

Doing

Cooking

TO FREEZE | DOUBLE UP

.... ◯◯

.... ◯◯

.... ◯◯

.... ◯◯

Eating

FROZEN | FRESH

.... ◯◯

.... ◯◯

.... ◯◯

.... ◯◯

Doing

....

....

Cooking

TO FREEZE | DOUBLE UP

.... ◯◯

.... ◯◯

.... ◯◯

.... ◯◯

Eating

FROZEN | FRESH

.... ◯◯

.... ◯◯

.... ◯◯

.... ◯◯

Doing

....

....

THURSDAY

Cooking	TO FREEZE	DOUBLE UP
....	◯	◯
....	◯	◯
....	◯	◯
....	◯	◯

Eating	FRESH	FROZEN
....	◯	◯
....	◯	◯
....	◯	◯
....	◯	◯

Doing

....

....

FRIDAY

Cooking	TO FREEZE	DOUBLE UP
....	◯	◯
....	◯	◯
....	◯	◯
....	◯	◯

Eating	FRESH	FROZEN
....	◯	◯
....	◯	◯
....	◯	◯
....	◯	◯

Doing

....

....

SATURDAY

Cooking

	TO FREEZE	DOUBLE UP
....	○	○
....	○	○
....	○	○
....	○	○

Eating

	FRESH	FROZEN
....	○	○
....	○	○
....	○	○
....	○	○

Doing

....
....

SUNDAY

Cooking

	TO FREEZE	DOUBLE UP
....	○	○
....	○	○
....	○	○
....	○	○

Eating

	FRESH	FROZEN
....	○	○
....	○	○
....	○	○
....	○	○

Doing

....
....

Shopping list

Once you've planned what you are going to be cooking and eating during the week, use the template below to make a shopping list of the ingredients that you need to buy. If you're planning to batch any of the meals for later, remember to scale up the ingredients accordingly. Before buying anything, remember to check the storecupboard and freezer lists at the end of this book (pp.234–255) to check off any ingredients that you already have to hand at home.

Fruit & Vegetables	QTY		QTY

Meat & Fish	QTY		QTY

Dairy QTY QTY

....

....

....

....

....

Storecupboard QTY QTY

....

....

....

....

....

Frozen Goods QTY QTY

....

....

....

....

....

Miscellaneous QTY QTY

....

....

....

VEGETABLE KORMA

This curry requires no chopping at all and is cooked and ready within 30 minutes. Packed with vegetables, this is a really healthy and wholesome dish, but still feels enough of a treat for a Friday 'fakeaway'.

PREP: 5 MINUTES
COOK: 20–25 MINUTES
SERVES 4

1 tbsp vegetable oil
1 tsp frozen chopped garlic
1 cup (115g) frozen chopped
  onions
145g korma curry paste
3 cups (345g) frozen sweet
  potato chunks
2 cups (220g) diced peppers
1 x 400g can chopped
  tomatoes
1 x 400g can coconut milk
1 small bunch of coriander,
  chopped, to serve
cooked basmati rice (see
  opposite) or naan breads, to
  serve

01 Heat the oil in a large pan over a medium heat, then add the chopped garlic and onions and cook, stirring, for about 1 minute, until soft.

02 Add the korma paste, chopped sweet potato, peppers, tomatoes and coconut milk to the pot and stir to combine. Bring the mixture to the boil, then reduce to a simmer and leave to cook for 15–20 minutes, until the vegetables are tender.

TO SERVE NOW: The curry is now ready to serve, scattered with fresh coriander and with rice or naan breads alongside.

TO FREEZE: Leave until completely cool, then ladle into a large, labelled freezer bag and freeze flat for up to 3 months.

TO COOK FROM FROZEN: Remove from the freezer and leave to completely defrost in the fridge. Once defrosted, tip the curry into a pan and reheat until piping hot. Serve as described in the *To Serve Now* section, above.

HOW TO COOK PERFECT RICE

Despite seeming simple, even the most experienced cooks can struggle to cook rice well. It's easy to either end up with far too much, or not to get the beautiful, fluffy grains you were hoping for. Follow the basic rules below and you should end up with perfect rice every time. Just remember that different varieties of rice have different cooking times, so always check the packet before you cook.

PREP: 5 MINUTES
COOK: TIMINGS VARY, SEE PACKET INSTRUCTIONS

rice
boiling water
1 tsp salt

Ratio: 2 cups (480ml) water to every 1 cup (240ml) of rice

01 Work out how much rice you want to cook, based on the fact that half a cup of uncooked rice feeds 1 person.

02 Using this ratio, work out how much boiling water you need and add it to a medium–large pan along with the salt (the size of the pan will depend on how much rice you are cooking).

03 Once the water is boiling, pour the rice into the pan and stir to stop it sticking to the bottom. Reduce the heat to a simmer and cook, stirring occasionally, until tender, following the packet instructions for timings (which will vary depending on what variety of rice you are using).

04 Drain through a colander and rinse through with boiling water to remove any excess starch. The rice is now ready to serve.

To see a picture of this recipe, visit
thebatchlady.com/mealplanner

WEEK 8

WEEK COMMENCING _ _ _ _ _ _ _ _ _ _ _ _ _

Notes

....

....

....

....

MONDAY

Cooking

	TO FREEZE	DOUBLE UP
....	O	O
....	O	O
....	O	O
....	O	O

Eating

	FRESH	FROZEN
....	O	O
....	O	O
....	O	O
....	O	O

Doing

....

....

Cooking

DOUBLE UP
TO FREEZE

.... ◯◯

.... ◯◯

.... ◯◯

.... ◯◯

Eating

FROZEN
FRESH

.... ◯◯

.... ◯◯

.... ◯◯

.... ◯◯

Doing

....

....

Cooking

DOUBLE UP
TO FREEZE

.... ◯◯

.... ◯◯

.... ◯◯

.... ◯◯

Eating

FROZEN
FRESH

.... ◯◯

.... ◯◯

.... ◯◯

.... ◯◯

Doing

....

....

THURSDAY

Cooking

	TO FREEZE	DOUBLE UP
....	○	○
....	○	○
....	○	○
....	○	○

Eating

	FRESH	FROZEN
....	○	○
....	○	○
....	○	○
....	○	○

Doing

....

....

FRIDAY

Cooking

	TO FREEZE	DOUBLE UP
....	○	○
....	○	○
....	○	○
....	○	○

Eating

	FRESH	FROZEN
....	○	○
....	○	○
....	○	○
....	○	○

Doing

....

....

SATURDAY

Cooking
DOUBLE UP
TO FREEZE

.... ◯◯

.... ◯◯

.... ◯◯

.... ◯◯

Eating
FROZEN
FRESH

.... ◯◯

.... ◯◯

.... ◯◯

.... ◯◯

Doing

....

....

SUNDAY

Cooking
DOUBLE UP
TO FREEZE

.... ◯◯

.... ◯◯

.... ◯◯

.... ◯◯

Eating
FROZEN
FRESH

.... ◯◯

.... ◯◯

.... ◯◯

.... ◯◯

Doing

....

....

Shopping list

Once you've planned what you are going to be cooking and eating during the week, use the template below to make a shopping list of the ingredients that you need to buy. If you're planning to batch any of the meals for later, remember to scale up the ingredients accordingly. Before buying anything, remember to check the storecupboard and freezer lists at the end of this book (pp.234–255) to check off any ingredients that you already have to hand at home.

Fruit & Vegetables	QTY		QTY
....	....	....	....
....	....	....	....
....	....	....	....
....	....	....	....
....	....	....	....
....	....	....	....

Meat & Fish	QTY		QTY
....	....	....	....
....	....	....	....
....	....	....	....
....	....	....	....
....	....	....	....
....	....	....	....

Dairy

QTY   QTY

....
....
....
....
....

Storecupboard

QTY   QTY

....
....
....
....
....

Frozen Goods

QTY   QTY

....
....
....
....
....

Miscellaneous

QTY   QTY

....
....
....

BASIC TOMATO SAUCE

A great tomato sauce is the starting point to so many dishes, so I like to make a big batch of this and freeze it in portions so that I always have some to hand. It can be used to dress pasta, top pizzas or fill calzones, as a base in chilli or Bolognese, or you can even add some spice to the mix and use it to top enchiladas or in a tomato-based curry.

PREP: 2 MINUTES
COOK: 15 MINUTES
SERVES 4

2 x 400g cans chopped
  tomatoes
1 x 500g carton passata
2 tbsp tomato purée
3 tsp dried oregano
1–2 tsp frozen chopped garlic
salt and freshly ground pepper

01 To make the sauce, simply put all the ingredients in a pan over a medium heat and leave to simmer, stirring occasionally, for 15 minutes, until thickened.

TO USE NOW: The sauce is now ready to be used. It is great for dressing pasta, topping pizzas or using as a base for dishes such as Bolognese or lasagne.

TO FREEZE: Set aside to cool completely, then transfer to a labelled freezer bag, seal and freeze flat for up to 3 months.

TO USE FROM FROZEN:
The sauce can be defrosted slowly in the fridge or more quickly in the microwave. Once defrosted, simply reheat till piping hot in a pan or in the microwave and use as described in the *To Use Now* section, above.

To see a picture of this recipe, visit
thebatchlady.com/mealplanner

YOU'RE DOING *Great*

WEEK 9

Notes

....

....

....

....

MONDAY

Cooking

DOUBLE UP
TO FREEZE

.... ◯ ◯

.... ◯ ◯

.... ◯ ◯

.... ◯ ◯

Eating

FROZEN
FRESH

.... ◯ ◯

.... ◯ ◯

.... ◯ ◯

.... ◯ ◯

Doing

....

....

TUESDAY

Cooking

	TO FREEZE	DOUBLE UP
....	○	○
....	○	○
....	○	○
....	○	○

Eating

	FRESH	FROZEN
....	○	○
....	○	○
....	○	○
....	○	○

Doing

....

....

WEDNESDAY

Cooking

	TO FREEZE	DOUBLE UP
....	○	○
....	○	○
....	○	○
....	○	○

Eating

	FRESH	FROZEN
....	○	○
....	○	○
....	○	○
....	○	○

Doing

....

....

THURSDAY

Cooking

DOUBLE UP
TO FREEZE

.... ○○

.... ○○

.... ○○

.... ○○

Eating

FROZEN
FRESH

.... ○○

.... ○○

.... ○○

.... ○○

Doing

....

....

FRIDAY

Cooking

DOUBLE UP
TO FREEZE

.... ○○

.... ○○

.... ○○

.... ○○

Eating

FROZEN
FRESH

.... ○○

.... ○○

.... ○○

.... ○○

Doing

....

....

Cooking

DOUBLE UP
TO FREEZE

○ ○

.... ○ ○

.... ○ ○

.... ○ ○

Eating

FROZEN
FRESH

○ ○

.... ○ ○

.... ○ ○

.... ○ ○

Doing

....

....

SUNDAY

Cooking

DOUBLE UP
TO FREEZE

○ ○

.... ○ ○

.... ○ ○

.... ○ ○

Eating

FROZEN
FRESH

○ ○

.... ○ ○

.... ○ ○

.... ○ ○

Doing

....

....

Shopping list

Once you've planned what you are going to be cooking and eating during the week, use the template below to make a shopping list of the ingredients that you need to buy. If you're planning to batch any of the meals for later, remember to scale up the ingredients accordingly. Before buying anything, remember to check the storecupboard and freezer lists at the end of this book (pp.234–255) to check off any ingredients that you already have to hand at home.

Fruit & Vegetables	QTY		QTY
....	......	....	......
....	......	....	......
....	......	....	......
....	......	....	......
....	......	....	......
....	......	....	......

Meat & Fish	QTY		QTY
....	......	....	......
....	......	....	......
....	......	....	......
....	......	....	......
....	......	....	......

Dairy   QTY   QTY

....

....

....

....

....

Storecupboard   QTY   QTY

....

....

....

....

....

Frozen Goods   QTY   QTY

....

....

....

....

....

Miscellaneous   QTY   QTY

....

....

....

HOW TO COOK PERFECT PASTA

Everyone's favourite comfort food, pasta is at the heart of so many of our best-loved dishes. If you're anything like me, you may find it impossible not to cook far too much pasta Every. Single. Time. Luckily, the technique outlined below will have you cooking just the right amount and guarantees perfect pasta, time and time again.

PREP: 5 MINUTES
COOK: TIMINGS VARY, SEE PACKET INSTRUCTIONS

pasta
boiling water
1 tsp salt

Ratio: 2 cups (480ml) boiling water to every 75g pasta

01 Work out how much pasta you want to cook, based on the fact that 75g of uncooked pasta feeds 1 person.

02 Using the ratio above, work out how much boiling water you need and add it to a medium–large pan along with the salt (the size of the pan will depend on how much pasta you are cooking).

03 Once the water is boiling, pour the pasta into the pan and stir to stop it sticking to the bottom. Reduce the heat to a simmer and cook, stirring occasionally, until tender, according to the packet instructions (timings vary depending on what variety of pasta you are using, though most varieties cook in 8–12 minutes).

04 Drain through a colander and rinse through with boiling water to remove any excess starch. The pasta is now ready to serve.

To see a picture of this recipe, visit
thebatchlady.com/mealplanner

DON'T BE
Busy,
BE
Productive!

WEEK 10

Notes

MONDAY

Cooking

DOUBLE UP
TO FREEZE

○○

○○

○○

○○

Eating

FROZEN
FRESH

○○

○○

○○

○○

Doing

Cooking

DOUBLE UP
TO FREEZE

.... ○ ○

.... ○ ○

.... ○ ○

.... ○ ○

Eating

FROZEN
FRESH

.... ○ ○

.... ○ ○

.... ○ ○

.... ○ ○

Doing

....

....

WEDNESDAY

Cooking

DOUBLE UP
TO FREEZE

.... ○ ○

.... ○ ○

.... ○ ○

.... ○ ○

Eating

FROZEN
FRESH

.... ○ ○

.... ○ ○

.... ○ ○

.... ○ ○

Doing

....

....

THURSDAY

Cooking

	TO FREEZE	DOUBLE UP
....	○	○
....	○	○
....	○	○
....	○	○

Eating

	FRESH	FROZEN
....	○	○
....	○	○
....	○	○
....	○	○

Doing

....

....

FRIDAY

Cooking

	TO FREEZE	DOUBLE UP
....	○	○
....	○	○
....	○	○
....	○	○

Eating

	FRESH	FROZEN
....	○	○
....	○	○
....	○	○
....	○	○

Doing

....

....

Cooking

	TO FREEZE	DOUBLE UP
....	◯	◯
....	◯	◯
....	◯	◯
....	◯	◯

Eating

	FROZEN	FRESH
....	◯	◯
....	◯	◯
....	◯	◯
....	◯	◯

Doing

....

....

Cooking

	TO FREEZE	DOUBLE UP
....	◯	◯
....	◯	◯
....	◯	◯
....	◯	◯

Eating

	FROZEN	FRESH
....	◯	◯
....	◯	◯
....	◯	◯
....	◯	◯

Doing

....

....

Shopping list

Once you've planned what you are going to be cooking and eating during the week, use the template below to make a shopping list of the ingredients that you need to buy. If you're planning to batch any of the meals for later, remember to scale up the ingredients accordingly. Before buying anything, remember to check the storecupboard and freezer lists at the end of this book (pp.234–255) to check off any ingredients that you already have to hand at home.

Fruit & Vegetables

	QTY		QTY
....	......	....	......
....	......	....	......
....	......	....	......
....	......	....	......
....	......	....	......
....	......	....	......
....	......	....	......

Meat & Fish

	QTY		QTY
....	......	....	......
....	......	....	......
....	......	....	......
....	......	....	......
....	......	....	......
....	......	....	......

Dairy QTY QTY

....
....
....
....
....

Storecupboard QTY QTY

....
....
....
....
....

Frozen Goods QTY QTY

....
....
....
....
....

Miscellaneous QTY QTY

....
....
....

CHEESE SAUCE

Equally at home used to dress macaroni or top a lasagne as it is spooned over baked meats or baked into cauliflower cheese, this is one of those recipes that every home cook should know how to make. This version freezes really well, so make a big batch and defrost as needed.

PREP: 15 MINUTES
**MAKES ABOUT
2½ CUPS (600ML)**

50g butter, cubed
4 tbsp plain flour
2½ cups (600ml) whole or
  semi-skimmed milk
2 cups (180g) pre-grated
  Cheddar cheese
1 tsp Dijon mustard (optional)

01 Heat the butter in a large pan over a medium heat, until melted, then add the flour and cook, stirring, until the mixture has come together and thickened. Pour in a little of the milk and cook, whisking continuously, until the liquid has thickened. Keep adding more of the milk to the pan, whisking and thickening between each addition, until all of the milk has been used up and you have a thick, glossy white sauce.

02 Remove the pan from the heat and add the cheese and Dijon mustard, if using, then whisk until the cheese has melted into the sauce.

TO USE NOW: The sauce is now ready to be used to make any number of dishes. It is great served over cooked chicken or baked in a cauliflower cheese. It can also be used to make moussaka, lasagne or macaroni cheese.

....

TO FREEZE: Set aside to cool completely, then ladle into a labelled freezer bag and freeze flat for up to 3 months.

....

TO USE FROM FROZEN: Remove the bag from the freezer and allow to defrost fully in the fridge, then reheat in a pan until bubbling and use as described in the *To Use Now* section, above.

To see a picture of this recipe, visit
thebatchlady.com/mealplanner

FREEZER RUNNING LOW?

Let's get
BATCHING!

WEEK 11

WEEK COMMENCING _____

Notes

....

....

....

....

MONDAY

Cooking

DOUBLE UP
TO FREEZE

.... ◯ ◯

.... ◯ ◯

.... ◯ ◯

.... ◯ ◯

Eating

FROZEN
FRESH

.... ◯ ◯

.... ◯ ◯

.... ◯ ◯

.... ◯ ◯

Doing

....

....

TUESDAY

Cooking

	TO FREEZE	DOUBLE UP
....	○	○
....	○	○
....	○	○
....	○	○

Eating

	FRESH	FROZEN
....	○	○
....	○	○
....	○	○
....	○	○

Doing

....

....

WEDNESDAY

Cooking

	TO FREEZE	DOUBLE UP
....	○	○
....	○	○
....	○	○
....	○	○

Eating

	FRESH	FROZEN
....	○	○
....	○	○
....	○	○
....	○	○

Doing

....

....

THURSDAY

Cooking

		TO FREEZE	DOUBLE UP
....		○	○
....		○	○
....		○	○
....		○	○

Eating

		FROZEN	FRESH
....		○	○
....		○	○
....		○	○
....		○	○

Doing

....

....

FRIDAY

Cooking

		TO FREEZE	DOUBLE UP
....		○	○
....		○	○
....		○	○
....		○	○

Eating

		FROZEN	FRESH
....		○	○
....		○	○
....		○	○
....		○	○

Doing

....

....

Cooking

DOUBLE UP
TO FREEZE

.... ○ ○

.... ○ ○

.... ○ ○

.... ○ ○

Eating

FROZEN
FRESH

.... ○ ○

.... ○ ○

.... ○ ○

.... ○ ○

Doing

....

....

Cooking

DOUBLE UP
TO FREEZE

.... ○ ○

.... ○ ○

.... ○ ○

.... ○ ○

Eating

FROZEN
FRESH

.... ○ ○

.... ○ ○

.... ○ ○

.... ○ ○

Doing

....

....

Shopping list

Once you've planned what you are going to be cooking and eating during the week, use the template below to make a shopping list of the ingredients that you need to buy. If you're planning to batch any of the meals for later, remember to scale up the ingredients accordingly. Before buying anything, remember to check the storecupboard and freezer lists at the end of this book (pp.234–255) to check off any ingredients that you already have to hand at home.

Fruit & Vegetables	QTY		QTY
....	......	....	......
....	......	....	......
....	......	....	......
....	......	....	......
....	......	....	......
....	......	....	......
....	......	....	......

Meat & Fish	QTY		QTY
....	......	....	......
....	......	....	......
....	......	....	......
....	......	....	......
....	......	....	......
....	......	....	......

Dairy   QTY   QTY

....
....
....
....
....

Storecupboard   QTY   QTY

....
....
....
....
....
....

Frozen Goods   QTY   QTY

....
....
....
....
....

Miscellaneous   QTY   QTY

....
....
....

RATATOUILLE

PREP: 5 MINUTES
COOK: 25 MINUTES
SERVES 4

1 tbsp olive oil
2 x 400g packs fresh
  Mediterranean-style
  vegetables
1 aubergine, cut into 2cm
  (¾in) cubes
1 tsp frozen chopped garlic
2 x 400g cans chopped
  tomatoes
1 tsp dried oregano
1 tbsp tomato purée
1 tsp sugar
salt and freshly ground pepper
couscous, to serve

01 Heat the oil in a large saucepan over a medium heat, then add the Mediterranean vegetables, cubed aubergines and garlic. Cook for 5 minutes, stirring occasionally, until starting to soften, then add the chopped tomatoes, oregano, tomato purée, sugar and a grinding of salt and pepper.

02 Bring the mixture to a boil, then reduce to a gentle simmer and leave to cook for 20 minutes until the sauce has thickened and the vegetables are tender.

03 Bring the saucepan to the boil and then reduce the heat and allow the ratatouille to cook for around 20 minutes, until the sauce has thickened and the vegetables are soft.

TO SERVE NOW: Spoon the ratatouille into bowls and serve hot with couscous alongside, if you like.

TO FREEZE: Leave the ratatouille until completely cooled, then ladle into a large, labelled freezer bag and freeze flat for up to 3 months.

TO COOK FROM FROZEN: Remove from the freezer and allow to completely defrost in the fridge. Once defrosted, tip the ratatouille into a large pan over a medium heat and cook, stirring occasionally, for 5–10 minutes, until piping hot. Serve.

HOW TO COOK PERFECT COUSCOUS

Couscous makes a wonderful, healthy side dish to any Middle Eastern-style recipe and has the added bonus of being really quick to make. You can enjoy it plain or spike it with as many herbs and spices as you like. Plus, it is delicious hot or cold, so it really is very versatile. Below is my method for making perfect couscous; master this basic method and you can start to play with your own spice mixes and flavours and be sure of great results every time.

PREP: 10 MINUTES

couscous
boiling water
1 tbsp olive oil, optional

Ratio: 1 cup (240ml) boiling water to every 1 cup of couscous

01 Work out how much couscous you want to cook, based on the fact that half a cup of uncooked couscous feeds 1 person.

02 Put the couscous in a heatproof bowl, then using the ratio above, work out how much boiling water you need and pour it over the couscous. Stir once to ensure all the grains are submerged.

03 Cover with a clean tea towel and set aside for 10 minutes until tender and all of the liquid has been absorbed.

04 Fluff the couscous up with a fork. The couscous is now ready to serve. If you want to serve it cooled, stir through the olive oil to prevent it sticking and set aside to cool.

To see a picture of this recipe, visit
thebatchlady.com/mealplanner

WEEK 12

Notes

....
....
....
....

MONDAY

Cooking

DOUBLE UP TO FREEZE

.... ○○
.... ○○
.... ○○
.... ○○

Eating

FROZEN FRESH

.... ○○
.... ○○
.... ○○
.... ○○

Doing

....
....

Cooking

TO FREEZE DOUBLE UP

.... ○○

.... ○○

.... ○○

.... ○○

Eating

FROZEN FRESH

.... ○○

.... ○○

.... ○○

.... ○○

Doing

....

....

Cooking

TO FREEZE DOUBLE UP

.... ○○

.... ○○

.... ○○

.... ○○

Eating

FROZEN FRESH

.... ○○

.... ○○

.... ○○

.... ○○

Doing

....

....

THURSDAY

Cooking

TO FREEZE DOUBLE UP

.... ○ ○

.... ○ ○

.... ○ ○

.... ○ ○

Eating

FROZEN FRESH

.... ○ ○

.... ○ ○

.... ○ ○

.... ○ ○

Doing

....

....

FRIDAY

Cooking

TO FREEZE DOUBLE UP

.... ○ ○

.... ○ ○

.... ○ ○

.... ○ ○

Eating

FROZEN FRESH

.... ○ ○

.... ○ ○

.... ○ ○

.... ○ ○

Doing

....

....

SATURDAY

Cooking
	TO FREEZE	DOUBLE UP
....	○	○
....	○	○
....	○	○
....	○	○

Eating
	FRESH	FROZEN
....	○	○
....	○	○
....	○	○
....	○	○

Doing
....
....

SUNDAY

Cooking
	TO FREEZE	DOUBLE UP
....	○	○
....	○	○
....	○	○
....	○	○

Eating
	FRESH	FROZEN
....	○	○
....	○	○
....	○	○
....	○	○

Doing
....
....

Shopping list

Once you've planned what you are going to be cooking and eating during the week, use the template below to make a shopping list of the ingredients that you need to buy. If you're planning to batch any of the meals for later, remember to scale up the ingredients accordingly. Before buying anything, remember to check the storecupboard and freezer lists at the end of this book (pp.234–255) to check off any ingredients that you already have to hand at home.

Fruit & Vegetables	QTY		QTY
....	......	....	......
....	......	....	......
....	......	....	......
....	......	....	......
....	......	....	......
....	......	....	......

Meat & Fish	QTY		QTY
....	......	....	......
....	......	....	......
....	......	....	......
....	......	....	......
....	......	....	......

Dairy   QTY   QTY

....

....

....

....

....

Storecupboard   QTY   QTY

....

....

....

....

....

....

Frozen Goods   QTY   QTY

....

....

....

....

....

Miscellaneous   QTY   QTY

....

....

....

TUNA & SWEETCORN GNOCCHI BAKE

Gnocchi is a wonderful alternative to pasta, though it is often overlooked or dismissed as being complicated or time-consuming. In fact, nothing could be further from the truth, and this comforting dish of baked gnocchi couldn't be easier!

PREP: 5–10 MINUTES
COOK: 20–25 MINUTES
SERVES 4

1 tbsp butter
3 tbsp plain flour
3 cups (720ml) milk
½ cup (45g) pre-grated
  Cheddar cheese
1 x 325g can sweetcorn,
  drained
2 x 160g cans tuna, drained
1 x 500g pack gnocchi
½ cup (45g) panko
  breadcrumbs

01 Heat the butter in a large pan over a medium heat until melted, then add the flour and cook, stirring, until the mixture has come together and thickened. Pour in a little of the milk and cook, whisking continuously, until the liquid thickens. Keep adding more, whisking and thickening between each addition, until all of the milk has been used up and you have a thick, glossy white sauce.

02 Remove the pan from the heat and add the cheese and sweetcorn, then flake in the tuna and stir to combine. Set aside while you cook the gnocchi.

To see a picture of this recipe, visit
thebatchlady.com/mealplanner

03 Bring a large pan of water to the boil, tip in the gnocchi and reduce the heat to a simmer. Cook for 3–4 minutes, until all the gnocchi have floated to the top of the pan. Drain through a colander and leave to steam dry for 1 minute.

04 Add the gnocchi to the pan with the tuna and sweetcorn sauce and stir until everything is well combined, then tip the mixture into a large baking dish and scatter over the panko breadcrumbs.

TO COOK NOW: Transfer the baking dish to an oven preheated to 180°C/350°F/gas mark 4 and leave to cook for 20–25 minutes until golden brown and bubbling. Serve hot.

TO FREEZE: Set aside to cool completely, then put the lid on the baking dish, if it has one, or wrap it in a layer of clingfilm followed by a layer of foil, label and transfer to the freezer for up to 3 months.

TO COOK FROM FROZEN: This can be cooked straight from the freezer. Remove the lid or foil and clingfilm and transfer to an oven preheated to 180°C/350°F/gas mark 4 for 30–35 minutes, until golden, bubbling and piping hot all the way through. Serve hot.

Tip

To make this even quicker, you could make this with a batch of cheese sauce from the freezer (p.100). If you do this, the bake must be eaten on the day and cannot be refrozen.

Batch Day

DATE

Use this page to plan for the days when you want to tackle a dedicated batching session, making several meals at once to fill your freezer. Write a list of the meals that you want to make below, making sure to mark if you're planning to double up any of the recipes. Once you've planned what you're going to cook, use the shopping list opposite to write down what you need to buy. I like to do a special visit to the shops or order online when planning a batch day, as that way I can lay everything out on the sides when I get home and am ready to start, without having to scrabble around in the cupboards trying to find things while I'm cooking.

What I'm cooking

Double Up

.... ○
.... ○
.... ○
.... ○
.... ○
.... ○
.... ○
.... ○
.... ○

Notes

....
....
....

BATCH DAY SHOPPING LIST

Fruit & Vegetables	QTY		QTY
....	......	....	......
....	......	....	......
....	......	....	......
....	......	....	......

Meat & Fish	QTY		QTY
....	......	....	......
....	......	....	......
....	......	....	......
....	......	....	......

Dairy	QTY		QTY
....	......	....	......
....	......	....	......
....	......	....	......
....	......	....	......

Storecupboard	QTY		QTY
....	......	....	......
....	......	....	......
....	......	....	......

Frozen Goods	QTY		QTY
....	......	....	......
....	......	....	......
....	......	....	......

WEEK 13

Notes

....

....

....

....

MONDAY

Cooking

DOUBLE UP
TO FREEZE

.... ○ ○

.... ○ ○

.... ○ ○

.... ○ ○

Eating

FROZEN
FRESH

.... ○ ○

.... ○ ○

.... ○ ○

.... ○ ○

Doing

....

....

Cooking

DOUBLE UP
TO FREEZE

.... ◯ ◯

.... ◯ ◯

.... ◯ ◯

.... ◯ ◯

Eating

FROZEN
FRESH

.... ◯ ◯

.... ◯ ◯

.... ◯ ◯

.... ◯ ◯

Doing

....

....

WEDNESDAY

Cooking

DOUBLE UP
TO FREEZE

.... ◯ ◯

.... ◯ ◯

.... ◯ ◯

.... ◯ ◯

Eating

FROZEN
FRESH

.... ◯ ◯

.... ◯ ◯

.... ◯ ◯

.... ◯ ◯

Doing

....

....

THURSDAY

Cooking
DOUBLE UP
TO FREEZE

.... ○ ○

.... ○ ○

.... ○ ○

.... ○ ○

Eating
FROZEN
FRESH

.... ○ ○

.... ○ ○

.... ○ ○

.... ○ ○

Doing

....

....

FRIDAY

Cooking
DOUBLE UP
TO FREEZE

.... ○ ○

.... ○ ○

.... ○ ○

.... ○ ○

Eating
FROZEN
FRESH

.... ○ ○

.... ○ ○

.... ○ ○

.... ○ ○

Doing

....

....

Cooking

DOUBLE UP
TO FREEZE

.... ○ ○

.... ○ ○

.... ○ ○

.... ○ ○

Eating

FROZEN
FRESH

.... ○ ○

.... ○ ○

.... ○ ○

.... ○ ○

Doing

....

....

SUNDAY

Cooking

DOUBLE UP
TO FREEZE

.... ○ ○

.... ○ ○

.... ○ ○

.... ○ ○

Eating

FROZEN
FRESH

.... ○ ○

.... ○ ○

.... ○ ○

.... ○ ○

Doing

....

....

Shopping list

Once you've planned what you are going to be cooking and eating during the week, use the template below to make a shopping list of the ingredients that you need to buy. If you're planning to batch any of the meals for later, remember to scale up the ingredients accordingly. Before buying anything, remember to check the storecupboard and freezer lists at the end of this book (pp.234–255) to check off any ingredients that you already have to hand at home.

Fruit & Vegetables	QTY		QTY
....	......	....	......
....	......	....	......
....	......	....	......
....	......	....	......
....	......	....	......
....	......	....	......
....	......	....	......

Meat & Fish	QTY		QTY
....	......	....	......
....	......	....	......
....	......	....	......
....	......	....	......
....	......	....	......
....	......	....	......

Dairy

	QTY		QTY
....	......	....	......
....	......	....	......
....	......	....	......
....	......	....	......

Storecupboard

	QTY		QTY
....	......	....	......
....	......	....	......
....	......	....	......
....	......	....	......
....	......	....	......
....	......	....	......

Frozen Goods

	QTY		QTY
....	......	....	......
....	......	....	......
....	......	....	......
....	......	....	......
....	......	....	......

Miscellaneous

	QTY		QTY
....	......	....	......
....	......	....	......
....	......	....	......

HOW TO COOK PERFECT GNOCCHI

Gnocchi makes a great alternative to rice, pasta and potatoes and is definitely worth adding to your weekly meal plan. Though it is actually made from potato, you will find it with the fresh pasta at the supermarket. If you're new to cooking gnocchi, follow the method below for perfect results every time.

PREP: 1 MINUTE
COOK: 2–4 MINUTES

gnocchi
boiling water
1 tsp salt

Ratio: 2 cups (480ml) boiling water to every 125g gnocchi

01 Work out how much gnocchi you want to cook, based on the fact that 125g of uncooked gnocchi feeds 1 person.

02 Using the ratio above, work out how much boiling water you need and add it to a medium–large pan along with the salt (the size of the pan will depend on how much gnocchi you are cooking).

03 Once the water is boiling, add the gnocchi to the pan and stir to stop it sticking to the bottom. Reduce the heat to a simmer and cook for 2–4 minutes, until all the gnocchi floats to the surface of the water.

04 Drain through a colander and rinse through with boiling water to remove any excess starch. The gnocchi is now ready to serve.

To see a picture of this recipe, visit
thebatchlady.com/mealplanner

Week PLANNED?

TIME FOR Fun!

WEEK 14

Notes

....

....

....

....

MONDAY

Cooking

	DOUBLE UP TO FREEZE
....	◯ ◯
....	◯ ◯
....	◯ ◯
....	◯ ◯

Eating

	FROZEN FRESH
....	◯ ◯
....	◯ ◯
....	◯ ◯
....	◯ ◯

Doing

....

....

Cooking

TO FREEZE · DOUBLE UP

.... ◯◯

.... ◯◯

.... ◯◯

.... ◯◯

Eating

FRESH · FROZEN

.... ◯◯

.... ◯◯

.... ◯◯

.... ◯◯

Doing

....

....

Cooking

TO FREEZE · DOUBLE UP

.... ◯◯

.... ◯◯

.... ◯◯

.... ◯◯

Eating

FRESH · FROZEN

.... ◯◯

.... ◯◯

.... ◯◯

.... ◯◯

Doing

....

....

THURSDAY

Cooking
TO FREEZE | DOUBLE UP

.... ◯ ◯

.... ◯ ◯

.... ◯ ◯

.... ◯ ◯

Eating
FROZEN | FRESH

.... ◯ ◯

.... ◯ ◯

.... ◯ ◯

.... ◯ ◯

Doing

....

....

FRIDAY

Cooking
TO FREEZE | DOUBLE UP

.... ◯ ◯

.... ◯ ◯

.... ◯ ◯

.... ◯ ◯

Eating
FROZEN | FRESH

.... ◯ ◯

.... ◯ ◯

.... ◯ ◯

.... ◯ ◯

Doing

....

....

SATURDAY

Cooking

	DOUBLE UP	TO FREEZE
....	○	○
....	○	○
....	○	○
....	○	○

Eating

	FROZEN	FRESH
....	○	○
....	○	○
....	○	○
....	○	○

Doing

....

....

SUNDAY

Cooking

	DOUBLE UP	TO FREEZE
....	○	○
....	○	○
....	○	○
....	○	○

Eating

	FROZEN	FRESH
....	○	○
....	○	○
....	○	○
....	○	○

Doing

....

....

Shopping list

Once you've planned what you are going to be cooking and eating during the week, use the template below to make a shopping list of the ingredients that you need to buy. If you're planning to batch any of the meals for later, remember to scale up the ingredients accordingly. Before buying anything, remember to check the storecupboard and freezer lists at the end of this book (pp.234–255) to check off any ingredients that you already have to hand at home.

Fruit & Vegetables	QTY		QTY

Meat & Fish	QTY		QTY

Dairy	QTY		QTY
⋯⋯⋯⋯⋯⋯⋯	⋯⋯	⋯⋯⋯⋯⋯⋯⋯⋯⋯⋯⋯	⋯⋯
⋯⋯⋯⋯⋯⋯⋯	⋯⋯	⋯⋯⋯⋯⋯⋯⋯⋯⋯⋯⋯	⋯⋯
⋯⋯⋯⋯⋯⋯⋯	⋯⋯	⋯⋯⋯⋯⋯⋯⋯⋯⋯⋯⋯	⋯⋯
⋯⋯⋯⋯⋯⋯⋯	⋯⋯	⋯⋯⋯⋯⋯⋯⋯⋯⋯⋯⋯	⋯⋯
⋯⋯⋯⋯⋯⋯⋯	⋯⋯	⋯⋯⋯⋯⋯⋯⋯⋯⋯⋯⋯	⋯⋯

Storecupboard	QTY		QTY
⋯⋯⋯⋯⋯⋯⋯	⋯⋯	⋯⋯⋯⋯⋯⋯⋯⋯⋯⋯⋯	⋯⋯
⋯⋯⋯⋯⋯⋯⋯	⋯⋯	⋯⋯⋯⋯⋯⋯⋯⋯⋯⋯⋯	⋯⋯
⋯⋯⋯⋯⋯⋯⋯	⋯⋯	⋯⋯⋯⋯⋯⋯⋯⋯⋯⋯⋯	⋯⋯
⋯⋯⋯⋯⋯⋯⋯	⋯⋯	⋯⋯⋯⋯⋯⋯⋯⋯⋯⋯⋯	⋯⋯
⋯⋯⋯⋯⋯⋯⋯	⋯⋯	⋯⋯⋯⋯⋯⋯⋯⋯⋯⋯⋯	⋯⋯

Frozen Goods	QTY		QTY
⋯⋯⋯⋯⋯⋯⋯	⋯⋯	⋯⋯⋯⋯⋯⋯⋯⋯⋯⋯⋯	⋯⋯
⋯⋯⋯⋯⋯⋯⋯	⋯⋯	⋯⋯⋯⋯⋯⋯⋯⋯⋯⋯⋯	⋯⋯
⋯⋯⋯⋯⋯⋯⋯	⋯⋯	⋯⋯⋯⋯⋯⋯⋯⋯⋯⋯⋯	⋯⋯
⋯⋯⋯⋯⋯⋯⋯	⋯⋯	⋯⋯⋯⋯⋯⋯⋯⋯⋯⋯⋯	⋯⋯
⋯⋯⋯⋯⋯⋯⋯	⋯⋯	⋯⋯⋯⋯⋯⋯⋯⋯⋯⋯⋯	⋯⋯

Miscellaneous	QTY		QTY
⋯⋯⋯⋯⋯⋯⋯	⋯⋯	⋯⋯⋯⋯⋯⋯⋯⋯⋯⋯⋯	⋯⋯
⋯⋯⋯⋯⋯⋯⋯	⋯⋯	⋯⋯⋯⋯⋯⋯⋯⋯⋯⋯⋯	⋯⋯
⋯⋯⋯⋯⋯⋯⋯	⋯⋯	⋯⋯⋯⋯⋯⋯⋯⋯⋯⋯⋯	⋯⋯

GARLIC & HERB STUFFED CHICKEN BREASTS

These chicken breasts are packed with flavour and are made from just three ingredients. Pair them with whatever veg you have that needs using up in your fridge for a speedy and nutritious midweek meal.

PREP: 5 MINUTES
COOK: 20–25 MINUTES
SERVES 4

4 skinless, boneless chicken breasts
100g garlic and herb cream cheese
8 slices Parma ham
cooked vegetables of your choice, to serve

01 Cut a small pocket into each of the chicken breasts by pushing the sharp point of a small knife into the fattest end of each piece, until the knife is about halfway down the length of the breast.

02 Fill each pocket with a quarter of the cream cheese, then wrap each piece of chicken with two slices of Parma ham.

To see a picture of this recipe, visit
thebatchlady.com/mealplanner

TO COOK NOW: Place the chicken on a foil-lined baking tray and transfer to an oven preheated to 170°C/325°F/gas mark 3 for 20–25 minutes, until the ham is beautifully crisp and the chicken is cooked through. Serve hot, with your choice of vegetables alongside.

....

TO FREEZE: Lay a large sheet of foil on the counter and place the uncooked, prepared chicken breasts on one half, then fold over the other half of the sheet of foil and crimp the edges together to form a parcel. Place the parcel in a large, labelled freezer bag and freeze flat for up to 3 months.

....

TO COOK FROM FROZEN: Remove from the freezer and leave to defrost thoroughly in the foil parcel in the fridge. Once defrosted, transfer to a baking tray and open the parcel slightly to allow hot air to escape while cooking. Cook as described in the *To Cook Now* section, left.

Zhuzh it up!
Once you've mastered this, why not try other fillings? Stilton and spinach or mascarpone and thyme would both work well.

WEEK 15

WEEK COMMENCING _ _ _ _ _ _ _ _ _ _ _ _ _ _ _

Notes

....

....

....

....

MONDAY

Cooking

	TO FREEZE	DOUBLE UP
....	○	○
....	○	○
....	○	○
....	○	○

Eating

	FRESH	FROZEN
....	○	○
....	○	○
....	○	○
....	○	○

Doing

....

....

Cooking — DOUBLE UP / TO FREEZE

.... ○ ○

.... ○ ○

.... ○ ○

.... ○ ○

Eating — FROZEN / FRESH

.... ○ ○

.... ○ ○

.... ○ ○

.... ○ ○

Doing

....

....

WEDNESDAY

Cooking — DOUBLE UP / TO FREEZE

.... ○ ○

.... ○ ○

.... ○ ○

.... ○ ○

Eating — FROZEN / FRESH

.... ○ ○

.... ○ ○

.... ○ ○

.... ○ ○

Doing

....

....

THURSDAY

Cooking

.... ○ ○

.... ○ ○

.... ○ ○

.... ○ ○

Eating

.... ○ ○

.... ○ ○

.... ○ ○

.... ○ ○

Doing

....

....

FRIDAY

Cooking

.... ○ ○

.... ○ ○

.... ○ ○

.... ○ ○

Eating

.... ○ ○

.... ○ ○

.... ○ ○

.... ○ ○

Doing

....

....

SATURDAY

Cooking

	DOUBLE UP	TO FREEZE
....	○	○
....	○	○
....	○	○
....	○	○

Eating

	FROZEN	FRESH
....	○	○
....	○	○
....	○	○
....	○	○

Doing

....

....

SUNDAY

Cooking

	DOUBLE UP	TO FREEZE
....	○	○
....	○	○
....	○	○
....	○	○

Eating

	FROZEN	FRESH
....	○	○
....	○	○
....	○	○
....	○	○

Doing

....

....

Shopping list

Once you've planned what you are going to be cooking and eating during the week, use the template below to make a shopping list of the ingredients that you need to buy. If you're planning to batch any of the meals for later, remember to scale up the ingredients accordingly. Before buying anything, remember to check the storecupboard and freezer lists at the end of this book (pp.234–255) to check off any ingredients that you already have to hand at home.

Fruit & Vegetables QTY QTY

....
....
....
....
....
....

Meat & Fish QTY QTY

....
....
....
....
....
....

Dairy	QTY		QTY

Storecupboard	QTY		QTY

Frozen Goods	QTY		QTY

Miscellaneous	QTY		QTY

CHEESY SAUSAGE ROLLS

These tasty sausage rolls can be cooked from frozen, so I like to make a big batch and pull them out of the freezer as needed. They are always a big hit at children's parties, as much with the adults as with the kids!

PREP: 10 MINUTES
COOK: 15 MINUTES
MAKES 16

6 pork sausages (approx. 400g)
1 cup (90g) pre-grated Cheddar cheese
1 sheet ready-rolled puff pastry
splash of milk
salt and freshly ground pepper

01 Slice open the sausages and turn the meat out into a large bowl, discarding the skins. Add the cheese to the bowl along with a generous grinding of salt and pepper, then use your hands to thoroughly combine the mixture.

02 Unroll the sheet of puff pastry and cut it in half lengthways, leaving you with 2 long, thin strips. Divide the sausage mixture between the two sheets, creating a line of the mixture down the centre third of each strip of pastry. Working with one piece of pastry at a time, fold one of the long edges of pastry over the sausage meat mixture to meet the other edge, then press together with a fork to seal all the way along the join.

03 Cut each long roll into 8 equal-sized pieces, leaving you with 16 sausage rolls.

To see a picture of this recipe, visit **thebatchlady.com/mealplanner**

TO COOK NOW: Place the sausage rolls on a baking tray lined with greaseproof paper, then brush the top of each roll with a little milk. Transfer to an oven preheated to 170°C/325°F/gas mark 3 and bake for 15 minutes, until the pastry is puffed and golden brown. These can be eaten warm from the oven or cooled and served at room temperature.

TO FREEZE: Transfer the unbaked rolls to a labelled freezer bag and freeze for up to 3 months.

TO COOK FROM FROZEN: These can be cooked straight from the freezer. Simply place the sausage rolls on a baking tray lined with greaseproof paper, then brush the top of each roll with a little milk. Transfer to an oven preheated to 170°C/325°F/gas mark 3 and bake for 30–35 minutes, until the pastry is puffed and golden brown and the sausage meat is piping hot. These can be eaten warm from the oven or cooled and served at room temperature.

Zhuzh it up!
For a spark of sweetness, lay thin slices of apple over the sausage meat before sealing the pastry.

WEEK 16

Notes

....
....
....
....

MONDAY

Cooking

	DOUBLE UP	TO FREEZE
....	○	○
....	○	○
....	○	○
....	○	○

Eating

	FROZEN	FRESH
....	○	○
....	○	○
....	○	○
....	○	○

Doing

....
....

Cooking

TO FREEZE | DOUBLE UP

.... ◯ ◯

.... ◯ ◯

.... ◯ ◯

.... ◯ ◯

Eating

FRESH | FROZEN

.... ◯ ◯

.... ◯ ◯

.... ◯ ◯

.... ◯ ◯

Doing

....

....

Cooking

TO FREEZE | DOUBLE UP

.... ◯ ◯

.... ◯ ◯

.... ◯ ◯

.... ◯ ◯

Eating

FRESH | FROZEN

.... ◯ ◯

.... ◯ ◯

.... ◯ ◯

.... ◯ ◯

Doing

....

....

THURSDAY

Cooking

	TO FREEZE	DOUBLE UP
....	○	○
....	○	○
....	○	○
....	○	○

Eating

	FRESH	FROZEN
....	○	○
....	○	○
....	○	○
....	○	○

Doing

....
....

FRIDAY

Cooking

	TO FREEZE	DOUBLE UP
....	○	○
....	○	○
....	○	○
....	○	○

Eating

	FRESH	FROZEN
....	○	○
....	○	○
....	○	○
....	○	○

Doing

....
....

Cooking

DOUBLE UP
TO FREEZE

.... ◯ ◯

.... ◯ ◯

.... ◯ ◯

.... ◯ ◯

Eating

FROZEN
FRESH

.... ◯ ◯

.... ◯ ◯

.... ◯ ◯

.... ◯ ◯

Doing

....

....

Cooking

DOUBLE UP
TO FREEZE

.... ◯ ◯

.... ◯ ◯

.... ◯ ◯

.... ◯ ◯

Eating

FROZEN
FRESH

.... ◯ ◯

.... ◯ ◯

.... ◯ ◯

.... ◯ ◯

Doing

....

....

Shopping list

Once you've planned what you are going to be cooking and eating during the week, use the template below to make a shopping list of the ingredients that you need to buy. If you're planning to batch any of the meals for later, remember to scale up the ingredients accordingly. Before buying anything, remember to check the storecupboard and freezer lists at the end of this book (pp.234–255) to check off any ingredients that you already have to hand at home.

Fruit & Vegetables	QTY		QTY

Meat & Fish	QTY		QTY

Dairy QTY QTY

....
....
....
....
....

Storecupboard QTY QTY

....
....
....
....
....
....

Frozen Goods QTY QTY

....
....
....
....
....

Miscellaneous QTY QTY

....
....
....

HOW TO COOK
PERFECT ORZO

Though it looks very much like large grains of rice, orzo is actually a delicious small pasta. It can be used in the same way as traditional pasta, but is also brilliant in salads or added to soups and stews to give bulk. The method below will help you work out how much orzo you need and show you how to cook your orzo perfectly.

PREP: 2 MINUTES
COOK: 8–10 MINUTES

orzo
boiling water
1 tsp salt

Ratio: 1¼ cups (300ml) boiling water to every 75g of orzo

01 Work out how much orzo you want to cook, based on the fact that 75g of uncooked orzo feeds 1 person.

02 Using the ratio above, work out how much boiling water you need and add it to medium–large pan along with the salt (the size of the pan will depend on how much orzo you are cooking).

03 Once the water is boiling, pour the orzo into the pan and stir to stop it sticking to the bottom. Reduce the heat to a simmer and cook, stirring occasionally, until tender, following the packet instructions from timings (which vary depending on what brand of orzo you are using, but it is generally cooked in 8–10 minutes).

04 Drain through a colander and rinse through with boiling water to remove any excess starch. The orzo is now ready to serve.

To see a picture of this recipe, visit
thebatchlady.com/mealplanner

GIVE YOURSELF A

night off!

WHAT'S
IN
THE
FREEZER?

WEEK 17

Notes

....

....

....

....

MONDAY

Cooking	TO FREEZE	DOUBLE UP
....	○	○
....	○	○
....	○	○
....	○	○

Eating	FRESH	FROZEN
....	○	○
....	○	○
....	○	○
....	○	○

Doing

....

....

Cooking

	TO FREEZE	DOUBLE UP
....	◯	◯
....	◯	◯
....	◯	◯
....	◯	◯

Eating

	FRESH	FROZEN
....	◯	◯
....	◯	◯
....	◯	◯
....	◯	◯

Doing

....

....

Cooking

	TO FREEZE	DOUBLE UP
....	◯	◯
....	◯	◯
....	◯	◯
....	◯	◯

Eating

	FRESH	FROZEN
....	◯	◯
....	◯	◯
....	◯	◯
....	◯	◯

Doing

....

....

THURSDAY

Cooking

TO FREEZE · DOUBLE UP

.... ○ ○

.... ○ ○

.... ○ ○

.... ○ ○

Eating

FRESH · FROZEN

.... ○ ○

.... ○ ○

.... ○ ○

.... ○ ○

Doing

....

....

FRIDAY

Cooking

TO FREEZE · DOUBLE UP

.... ○ ○

.... ○ ○

.... ○ ○

.... ○ ○

Eating

FRESH · FROZEN

.... ○ ○

.... ○ ○

.... ○ ○

.... ○ ○

Doing

....

....

SATURDAY

Cooking

TO FREEZE | DOUBLE UP

.... ○○

.... ○○

.... ○○

.... ○○

Eating

FRESH | FROZEN

.... ○○

.... ○○

.... ○○

.... ○○

Doing

....

....

SUNDAY

Cooking

TO FREEZE | DOUBLE UP

.... ○○

.... ○○

.... ○○

.... ○○

Eating

FRESH | FROZEN

.... ○○

.... ○○

.... ○○

.... ○○

Doing

....

....

Shopping list

Once you've planned what you are going to be cooking and eating during the week, use the template below to make a shopping list of the ingredients that you need to buy. If you're planning to batch any of the meals for later, remember to scale up the ingredients accordingly. Before buying anything, remember to check the storecupboard and freezer lists at the end of this book (pp.234–255) to check off any ingredients that you already have to hand at home.

Fruit & Vegetables	QTY		QTY

Meat & Fish	QTY		QTY

Believe
IN THE
BATCH

Miscellaneous

QTY

Baking Ingredients | QTY

Herbs & Spices

QTY

....

....

....

....

....

....

....

....

....

....

....

....

....

....

....

....

....

....

....

....

Herbs & Spices

QTY

....

....

....

....

....

....

....

....

....

....

....

....

....

....

....

....

....

....

....

....

Oils, Sauces & Vinegars   QTY

Oils, Sauces & Vinegars

QTY

Cans & Jars

QTY

Cans & Jars

QTY

Grains, Rice & Pasta | QTY

What's in the cupboard?

Grains, Rice & Pasta	QTY
....	....
....	....
....	....
....	....
....	....
....	....
....	....
....	....
....	....
....	....
....	....
....	....
....	....
....	....
....	....
....	....
....	....
....	....

Produce

Produce	Date Frozen	QTY

Produce	Date Frozen	QTY
....	....	....
....	....	....
....	....	....
....	....	....
....	....	....
....	....	....
....	....	....
....	....	....
....	....	....
....	....	....
....	....	....
....	....	....
....	....	....
....	....	....
....	....	....
....	....	....
....	....	....
....	....	....
....	....	....
....	....	....
....	....	....
....	....	....
....	....	....
....	....	....
....	....	....

Produce	Date Frozen	QTY

Produce   Date Frozen   QTY

....

....

....

....

....

....

....

....

....

....

....

....

....

....

....

....

....

....

....

....

....

....

Side Dishes

	Date Frozen	QTY

Side Dishes

	Date Frozen	QTY

Side Dishes

	Date Frozen	QTY

Side Dishes

	Date Frozen	QTY

Main Meals

	Date Frozen	QTY

Main Meals

	Date Frozen	QTY
....	....	....
....	....	....
....	....	....
....	....	....
....	....	....
....	....	....
....	....	....
....	....	....
....	....	....
....	....	....
....	....	....
....	....	....
....	....	....
....	....	....
....	....	....
....	....	....
....	....	....
....	....	....
....	....	....
....	....	....
....	....	....
....	....	....
....	....	....

Main Meals	Date Frozen	QTY
....	....	....
....	....	....
....	....	....
....	....	....
....	....	....
....	....	....
....	....	....
....	....	....
....	....	....
....	....	....
....	....	....
....	....	....
....	....	....
....	....	....
....	....	....
....	....	....
....	....	....
....	....	....
....	....	....
....	....	....
....	....	....
....	....	....

What's in the freezer?

Main Meals	Date Frozen	QTY
....	....	....
....	....	....
....	....	....
....	....	....
....	....	....
....	....	....
....	....	....
....	....	....
....	....	....
....	....	....
....	....	....
....	....	....
....	....	....
....	....	....
....	....	....
....	....	....
....	....	....
....	....	....
....	....	....

Dairy	QTY		QTY
....	......	....	......
....	......	....	......
....	......	....	......
....	......	....	......
....	......	....	......

Storecupboard	QTY		QTY
....	......	....	......
....	......	....	......
....	......	....	......
....	......	....	......
....	......	....	......

Frozen Goods	QTY		QTY
....	......	....	......
....	......	....	......
....	......	....	......
....	......	....	......
....	......	....	......

Miscellaneous	QTY		QTY
....	......	....	......
....	......	....	......
....	......	....	......

Dairy   QTY   QTY

....

....

....

....

....

Storecupboard   QTY   QTY

....

....

....

....

....

Frozen Goods   QTY   QTY

....

....

....

....

....

Miscellaneous   QTY   QTY

....

....

....

BREAKFAST PORRIDGE COOKIES

These cookies are packed full of goodness and are a brilliant standby for when you need a quick breakfast on the go. The recipe is easily adaptable, so feel free to mix up the nuts and seeds to use whatever you have to hand.

PREP: 5–10 MINUTES
COOK: 15 MINUTES
MAKES 8 LARGE COOKIES

2 cups (190g) porridge oats
4 tbsp maple syrup or runny honey
1 tsp ground cinnamon
½ cup (115g) peanut butter
½ cup (70g) pumpkin seeds
½ cup (65g) whole blanched almonds
½ cup (70g) raisins
2 ripe bananas
1 egg, beaten

01 Preheat the oven to 170°C/325°F/gas mark 3 and line a baking sheet with greaseproof paper.

02 In a large bowl, stir together the oats, maple syrup or honey, cinnamon, peanut butter, pumpkin seeds, blanched almonds and raisins until well combined.

03 In a separate bowl, mash the bananas with a fork, then add to the dry ingredients along with the beaten egg and stir again until all the ingredients are well combined.

To see a picture of this recipe, visit **thebatchlady.com/mealplanner**

04 Using an ice-cream scoop or large spoon, portion the mixture into 8 equal-sized balls and arrange on the prepared baking sheet, leaving a little space between each cookie to allow them to spread in the oven. Flatten each cookie slightly with your hands.

05 Transfer to the oven and leave to bake for 15 minutes, until golden. Remove from the oven and leave on the baking tray to firm up for 5 minutes, then transfer to a wire rack to finish cooling.

TO SERVE NOW: Once cooled, the cookies are ready to be served.

....

TO FREEZE: Once cooled, transfer the cookies to a large, labelled freezer bag in a single layer. Freeze flat for up to 3 months.

....

TO SERVE FROM FROZEN: Remove the cookies from the freezer and set on the counter to defrost. They should be ready to eat in around 30 minutes.

Zhuzh it up!
Try substituting pecans or walnuts for the almonds or adding chopped stem ginger to the mix for a fiery grown-up twist.

Batch Day

Use this page to plan for the days when you want to tackle a dedicated batching session, making several meals at once to fill your freezer. Write a list of the meals that you want to make below, making sure to mark if you're planning to double up any of the recipes. Once you've planned what you're going to cook, use the shopping list opposite to write down what you need to buy. I like to do a special visit to the shops or order online when planning a batch day, as that way I can lay everything out on the sides when I get home and am ready to start, without having to scrabble around in the cupboards trying to find things while I'm cooking.

DATE

- - - - - - - - - - - - - -

What I'm cooking

....

....

....

....

....

....

....

....

....

Double Up

○
○
○
○
○
○
○
○
○

Notes

....

....

....

BATCH DAY SHOPPING LIST

Fruit & Vegetables   QTY   QTY

....

....

....

....

Meat & Fish   QTY   QTY

....

....

....

....

Dairy   QTY   QTY

....

....

....

Storecupboard   QTY   QTY

....

....

....

Frozen Goods   QTY   QTY

....

....

....

WEEK 19

Notes

....

....

....

....

MONDAY

Cooking

	DOUBLE UP TO FREEZE
....	○ ○
....	○ ○
....	○ ○
....	○ ○

Eating

	FROZEN FRESH
....	○ ○
....	○ ○
....	○ ○
....	○ ○

Doing

....

....

Cooking

DOUBLE UP
TO FREEZE

.... ○ ○

.... ○ ○

.... ○ ○

.... ○ ○

Eating

FROZEN
FRESH

.... ○ ○

.... ○ ○

.... ○ ○

.... ○ ○

Doing

....

....

Cooking

DOUBLE UP
TO FREEZE

.... ○ ○

.... ○ ○

.... ○ ○

.... ○ ○

Eating

FROZEN
FRESH

.... ○ ○

.... ○ ○

.... ○ ○

.... ○ ○

Doing

....

....

THURSDAY

Cooking

DOUBLE UP
TO FREEZE

.... ○○

.... ○○

.... ○○

.... ○○

Eating

FROZEN
FRESH

.... ○○

.... ○○

.... ○○

.... ○○

Doing

....

....

FRIDAY

Cooking

DOUBLE UP
TO FREEZE

.... ○○

.... ○○

.... ○○

.... ○○

Eating

FROZEN
FRESH

.... ○○

.... ○○

.... ○○

.... ○○

Doing

....

....

SATURDAY

Cooking

DOUBLE UP
TO FREEZE

⭘⭘
....

⭘⭘
....

⭘⭘
....

⭘⭘
....

Eating

FROZEN
FRESH

⭘⭘
....

⭘⭘
....

⭘⭘
....

⭘⭘
....

Doing

....

....

SUNDAY

Cooking

DOUBLE UP
TO FREEZE

⭘⭘
....

⭘⭘
....

⭘⭘
....

⭘⭘
....

Eating

FROZEN
FRESH

⭘⭘
....

⭘⭘
....

⭘⭘
....

⭘⭘
....

Doing

....

....

Shopping list

Once you've planned what you are going to be cooking and eating during the week, use the template below to make a shopping list of the ingredients that you need to buy. If you're planning to batch any of the meals for later, remember to scale up the ingredients accordingly. Before buying anything, remember to check the storecupboard and freezer lists at the end of this book (pp.234–255) to check off any ingredients that you already have to hand at home.

Fruit & Vegetables	QTY		QTY

Meat & Fish	QTY		QTY

Dairy

	QTY		QTY
....	......	....	......
....	......	....	......
....	......	....	......
....	......	....	......
....	......	....	......

Storecupboard

	QTY		QTY
....	......	....	......
....	......	....	......
....	......	....	......
....	......	....	......
....	......	....	......
....	......	....	......

Frozen Goods

	QTY		QTY
....	......	....	......
....	......	....	......
....	......	....	......
....	......	....	......
....	......	....	......

Miscellaneous

	QTY		QTY
....	......	....	......
....	......	....	......
....	......	....	......

RATATOUILLE, HALLOUMI & PARMESAN BAKE

Another great twist on ratatouille, this baked version benefits from a delicious cheesy, crunchy top that transforms the dish into a real vegetarian showstopper.

PREP: 5 MINUTES
COOK: 1 HOUR
SERVES 4

1 tbsp olive oil
2 x 400g packs fresh
   Mediterranean-style
   vegetables
1 aubergine, cut into 2cm
   (¾in) cubes
1 tsp frozen chopped garlic
2 x 400g cans chopped
   tomatoes
1 tsp dried oregano
1 tbsp tomato purée
1 tsp sugar
1 x 225g halloumi cheese, cut
   into 5mm (¼in) slices
½ cup (50g) pre-grated
   Parmesan Cheese
½ cup (75g) white
   breadcrumbs
salt and freshly ground pepper

01 Heat the oil in a large saucepan over a medium heat, then add the Mediterranean vegetables, aubergine cubes and garlic. Cook for 5 minutes, stirring occasionally, until starting to soften, then add the chopped tomatoes, oregano, tomato purée, sugar and a grinding of salt and pepper.

02 Bring the mixture to a boil, then reduce to a gentle simmer and leave to cook for 20 minutes, until the sauce has thickened and the vegetables are tender.

03 Pour the ratatouille into a large baking dish and lay the halloumi slices over the top in an even layer, then sprinkle over the Parmesan cheese followed by the breadcrumbs.

TO COOK NOW: Transfer to an oven preheated to 180°C/350°F/gas mark 4 and bake for 25 minutes, until the top is golden brown and the sauce is bubbling. Serve hot.

....

TO FREEZE: Set aside until completely cooled, then cover the unbaked dish with a lid or wrap in a layer of clingfilm followed by a layer of foil, label and freeze flat for up to 3 months.

....

TO COOK FROM FROZEN:
Remove from the freezer and allow to completely defrost in the fridge. Once defrosted, transfer to an oven preheated to 180°C/350°F/gas mark 4 and bake for 30–40 minutes, until the top is golden brown and the sauce is bubbling. Serve hot.

Tip
If you have tomatoes, peppers, courgettes or red onions that need using up in the fridge, chop these up and use instead of the pre-packaged vegetables.

To see a picture of this recipe, visit **thebatchlady.com/mealplanner**

WEEK 21

Notes

....

....

....

....

MONDAY

Cooking

DOUBLE UP
TO FREEZE

.... ○ ○

.... ○ ○

.... ○ ○

.... ○ ○

Eating

FROZEN
FRESH

.... ○ ○

.... ○ ○

.... ○ ○

.... ○ ○

Doing

....

....

Cooking

DOUBLE UP
TO FREEZE

.... ○ ○

.... ○ ○

.... ○ ○

.... ○ ○

Eating

FROZEN
FRESH

.... ○ ○

.... ○ ○

.... ○ ○

.... ○ ○

Doing

....

....

Cooking

DOUBLE UP
TO FREEZE

.... ○ ○

.... ○ ○

.... ○ ○

.... ○ ○

Eating

FROZEN
FRESH

.... ○ ○

.... ○ ○

.... ○ ○

.... ○ ○

Doing

....

....

THURSDAY

Cooking

	DOUBLE UP	TO FREEZE
....	○	○
....	○	○
....	○	○
....	○	○

Eating

	FROZEN	FRESH
....	○	○
....	○	○
....	○	○
....	○	○

Doing

....

....

FRIDAY

Cooking

	DOUBLE UP	TO FREEZE
....	○	○
....	○	○
....	○	○
....	○	○

Eating

	FROZEN	FRESH
....	○	○
....	○	○
....	○	○
....	○	○

Doing

....

....

Cooking

DOUBLE UP
TO FREEZE

○○
○○
○○
○○

Eating

FROZEN
FRESH

○○
○○
○○
○○

Doing

Cooking

DOUBLE UP
TO FREEZE

○○
○○
○○
○○

Eating

FROZEN
FRESH

○○
○○
○○
○○

Doing

Shopping list

Once you've planned what you are going to be cooking and eating during the week, use the template below to make a shopping list of the ingredients that you need to buy. If you're planning to batch any of the meals for later, remember to scale up the ingredients accordingly. Before buying anything, remember to check the storecupboard and freezer lists at the end of this book (pp.234–255) to check off any ingredients that you already have to hand at home.

Fruit & Vegetables	QTY		QTY
....	......	....	......
....	......	....	......
....	......	....	......
....	......	....	......
....	......	....	......
....	......	....	......
....	......	....	......

Meat & Fish	QTY		QTY
....	......	....	......
....	......	....	......
....	......	....	......
....	......	....	......
....	......	....	......

Shopping list

Once you've planned what you are going to be cooking and eating during the week, use the template below to make a shopping list of the ingredients that you need to buy. If you're planning to batch any of the meals for later, remember to scale up the ingredients accordingly. Before buying anything, remember to check the storecupboard and freezer lists at the end of this book (pp.234–255) to check off any ingredients that you already have to hand at home.

Fruit & Vegetables	QTY		QTY
....	......	....	......
....	......	....	......
....	......	....	......
....	......	....	......
....	......	....	......
....	......	....	......
....	......	....	......

Meat & Fish	QTY		QTY
....	......	....	......
....	......	....	......
....	......	....	......
....	......	....	......
....	......	....	......

Cooking

DOUBLE UP
TO FREEZE

.... ○ ○

.... ○ ○

.... ○ ○

.... ○ ○

Eating

FROZEN
FRESH

.... ○ ○

.... ○ ○

.... ○ ○

.... ○ ○

Doing

....

....

Cooking

DOUBLE UP
TO FREEZE

.... ○ ○

.... ○ ○

.... ○ ○

.... ○ ○

Eating

FROZEN
FRESH

.... ○ ○

.... ○ ○

.... ○ ○

.... ○ ○

Doing

....

....

THURSDAY

Cooking

DOUBLE UP
TO FREEZE

.... ◯ ◯

.... ◯ ◯

.... ◯ ◯

.... ◯ ◯

Eating

FROZEN
FRESH

.... ◯ ◯

.... ◯ ◯

.... ◯ ◯

.... ◯ ◯

Doing

....

....

FRIDAY

Cooking

DOUBLE UP
TO FREEZE

.... ◯ ◯

.... ◯ ◯

.... ◯ ◯

.... ◯ ◯

Eating

FROZEN
FRESH

.... ◯ ◯

.... ◯ ◯

.... ◯ ◯

.... ◯ ◯

Doing

....

....

Cooking

	TO FREEZE	DOUBLE UP
....	○	○
....	○	○
....	○	○
....	○	○

Eating

	FRESH	FROZEN
....	○	○
....	○	○
....	○	○
....	○	○

Doing

....

....

Cooking

	TO FREEZE	DOUBLE UP
....	○	○
....	○	○
....	○	○
....	○	○

Eating

	FRESH	FROZEN
....	○	○
....	○	○
....	○	○
....	○	○

Doing

....

....

WEEK 20

Notes

....
....
....
....

MONDAY

Cooking

	TO FREEZE	DOUBLE UP
....	○	○
....	○	○
....	○	○
....	○	○

Eating

	FROZEN	FRESH
....	○	○
....	○	○
....	○	○
....	○	○

Doing

....
....

04 Transfer to the oven and bake for 15 minutes until golden and well risen.

05 Leave the muffins to cool slightly in the tin, then use a palette knife to transfer to a cooling rack.

Zhuzh it up!
Give them a zingy twist by adding the zest of a lemon to the mix. You could even make a glaze from the juice of half a lemon and a little icing sugar.

TO SERVE NOW: The muffins can be cooled to room temperature or eaten slightly warm from the oven. They are best eaten on the day they are made, but will keep in an airtight container for up to 2 days.

TO FREEZE: Leave the muffins to cool to room temperature, then transfer to a labelled freezer bag and freeze flat for up to 3 months.

TO SERVE FROM FROZEN: Remove the muffins from the freezer and set on the counter to defrost. They should be ready to eat in around 30 minutes.

BLUEBERRY MUFFINS

Whether enjoyed as an indulgent weekend breakfast, mid-morning pick-me-up or lunchbox treat, everyone loves a blueberry muffin. This recipe makes a batch of 12, so you can enjoy half on the day of baking and freeze the rest for later.

PREP: 10 MINUTES
COOK: 15 MINUTES
MAKES 12

½ cup (115g) butter, at room temperature
¾ cup (150g) caster sugar
3 eggs, beaten
1 tsp vanilla extract
1 cup (150g) self-raising flour
1 cup (125g) fresh blueberries

01 Preheat the oven to 170°C/325°F/gas mark 3 and line a 12-hole muffin tin with cases.

02 In a large bowl, cream the butter and caster sugar with an electric whisk until light and fluffy. Add the eggs and vanilla extract and whisk again to incorporate. Sift the flour into the mixture and whisk again until just combined.

03 Carefully fold the blueberries into the mixture with a wooden spoon, being careful not to break any of the fruit. Divide the mixture equally between the muffin cases, then tap the muffin tin on the counter to level out the mixture and remove any air bubbles.

To see a picture of this recipe, visit
thebatchlady.com/mealplanner

Dairy	QTY		QTY
....	......	....	......
....	......	....	......
....	......	....	......
....	......	....	......
....	......	....	......

Storecupboard	QTY		QTY
....	......	....	......
....	......	....	......
....	......	....	......
....	......	....	......
....	......	....	......

Frozen Goods	QTY		QTY
....	......	....	......
....	......	....	......
....	......	....	......
....	......	....	......
....	......	....	......

Miscellaneous	QTY		QTY
....	......	....	......
....	......	....	......
....	......	....	......

THURSDAY

Cooking
TO FREEZE / DOUBLE UP

.... ○○
.... ○○
.... ○○
.... ○○

Eating
FROZEN / FRESH

.... ○○
.... ○○
.... ○○
.... ○○

Doing

....
....

FRIDAY

Cooking
TO FREEZE / DOUBLE UP

.... ○○
.... ○○
.... ○○
.... ○○

Eating
FROZEN / FRESH

.... ○○
.... ○○
.... ○○
.... ○○

Doing

....
....

Cooking

DOUBLE UP
TO FREEZE

.... ○ ○

.... ○ ○

.... ○ ○

.... ○ ○

Eating

FROZEN
FRESH

.... ○ ○

.... ○ ○

.... ○ ○

.... ○ ○

Doing

....

....

WEDNESDAY

Cooking

DOUBLE UP
TO FREEZE

.... ○ ○

.... ○ ○

.... ○ ○

.... ○ ○

Eating

FROZEN
FRESH

.... ○ ○

.... ○ ○

.... ○ ○

.... ○ ○

Doing

....

....

WEEK 24

Notes

....

....

....

....

MONDAY

Cooking

	TO FREEZE	DOUBLE UP
....	○	○
....	○	○
....	○	○
....	○	○

Eating

	FRESH	FROZEN
....	○	○
....	○	○
....	○	○
....	○	○

Doing

....

....

TO COOK NOW: Transfer the baking dish to an oven preheated to 180°C/350°F/gas mark 4 for 45 minutes, until the chicken is cooked through, juicy and bubbling. Serve hot with noodles, pak choi or broccoli alongside.

....

TO FREEZE: Seal the freezer bag, squeezing out any excess air, transfer to the freezer and freeze flat for up to 3 months.

....

TO COOK FROM FROZEN: Remove from the freezer and allow to completely defrost in the fridge. Once defrosted, transfer to a shallow baking dish and cook as described in the *To Cook Now* section, above.

Tip

If you want to serve this with broccoli, lay the veg on top of the baking dish in the oven for the last 15 minutes of cooking time.

To see a picture of this recipe, visit
thebatchlady.com/mealplanner

STICKY ASIAN CHICKEN TRAYBAKE

This dish is packed with the vibrant flavours of Asia. It makes a wonderful accompaniment to noodles and possibly some beautifully fresh steamed greens, such as broccoli or pak choi. It's a great dish to make ahead and keep in the freezer as it can be assembled in moments, then cooked on the day you want to eat it.

PREP: 5–10 MINUTES
COOK: 45 MINUTES
SERVES 4

6–8 skin-on, bone-in chicken thighs
2 tbsp peanut butter
2 tbsp honey
5 tbsp soy sauce
1 tsp frozen chopped garlic
1 tsp frozen chopped ginger
4 spring onions, finely chopped
2 tbsp sweet chilli sauce
1 red chilli, finely chopped (optional)
noodles, pak choi or broccoli, to serve

01 Score the skin of each chicken thigh with a sharp knife – this allows the flavour of the marinade to permeate into the meat. If making the dish to serve straightaway, place the chicken thighs in a shallow baking dish in a single layer. If making ahead of time for the freezer, place the thighs in a large, labelled freezer bag.

02 Place the peanut butter, honey, soy sauce, garlic, ginger, spring onions, sweet chilli sauce and red chilli, if using, in a small bowl and stir to combine. Pour the marinade over the chicken, ensuring that the meat is well coated in the sauce.

Dairy QTY QTY

·········· ······ ·············· ······

·········· ······ ·············· ······

·········· ······ ·············· ······

·········· ······ ·············· ······

·········· ······ ·············· ······

Storecupboard QTY QTY

·········· ······ ·············· ······

·········· ······ ·············· ······

·········· ······ ·············· ······

·········· ······ ·············· ······

·········· ······ ·············· ······

Frozen Goods QTY QTY

·········· ······ ·············· ······

·········· ······ ·············· ······

·········· ······ ·············· ······

·········· ······ ·············· ······

·········· ······ ·············· ······

Miscellaneous QTY QTY

·········· ······ ·············· ······

·········· ······ ·············· ······

·········· ······ ·············· ······

Shopping list

Once you've planned what you are going to be cooking and eating during the week, use the template below to make a shopping list of the ingredients that you need to buy. If you're planning to batch any of the meals for later, remember to scale up the ingredients accordingly. Before buying anything, remember to check the storecupboard and freezer lists at the end of this book (pp.234–255) to check off any ingredients that you already have to hand at home.

Fruit & Vegetables	QTY		QTY
....	......	....	......
....	......	....	......
....	......	....	......
....	......	....	......
....	......	....	......
....	......	....	......
....	......	....	......

Meat & Fish	QTY		QTY
....	......	....	......
....	......	....	......
....	......	....	......
....	......	....	......
....	......	....	......
....	......	....	......

Cooking

	TO FREEZE	DOUBLE UP
....	○	○
....	○	○
....	○	○
....	○	○

Eating

	FRESH	FROZEN
....	○	○
....	○	○
....	○	○
....	○	○

Doing

....

....

Cooking

	TO FREEZE	DOUBLE UP
....	○	○
....	○	○
....	○	○
....	○	○

Eating

	FRESH	FROZEN
....	○	○
....	○	○
....	○	○
....	○	○

Doing

....

....

THURSDAY

Cooking

DOUBLE UP
TO FREEZE

.... ○○

.... ○○

.... ○○

.... ○○

Eating

FROZEN
FRESH

.... ○○

.... ○○

.... ○○

.... ○○

Doing

....

....

FRIDAY

Cooking

DOUBLE UP
TO FREEZE

.... ○○

.... ○○

.... ○○

.... ○○

Eating

FROZEN
FRESH

.... ○○

.... ○○

.... ○○

.... ○○

Doing

....

....

Cooking

DOUBLE UP
TO FREEZE

.... ○ ○

.... ○ ○

.... ○ ○

.... ○ ○

Eating

FROZEN
FRESH

.... ○ ○

.... ○ ○

.... ○ ○

.... ○ ○

Doing

....

....

Cooking

DOUBLE UP
TO FREEZE

.... ○ ○

.... ○ ○

.... ○ ○

.... ○ ○

Eating

FROZEN
FRESH

.... ○ ○

.... ○ ○

.... ○ ○

.... ○ ○

Doing

....

....

WEEK 23

WEEK COMMENCING _____

Notes

....

....

....

....

MONDAY

Cooking	TO FREEZE	DOUBLE UP
....	○	○
....	○	○
....	○	○
....	○	○

Eating	FRESH	FROZEN
....	○	○
....	○	○
....	○	○
....	○	○

Doing

....

....

THE

Secret

TO GETTING

Ahead

IS GETTING

Started!

LUXURIOUS
RICE PUDDING

There are few things more comforting than a bowl of deliciously rich rice pudding, and this decadent version is sure to be a hit with adults and children alike. This is delicious as it is, but for an extra touch of luxury you could top this with your choice of fresh berries to serve.

PREP: 5 MINUTES
COOK: 50 MINUTES
SERVES 4

⅔ cup (120g) pudding rice
50g butter
4 tbsp soft light brown sugar
3 tbsp caster sugar
3 cups (720ml) whole milk
½ cup (120ml) single cream
1 tsp vanilla essence

01 Put all of the ingredients in a large saucepan over a medium heat, then cook, stirring occasionally, until the mixture just starts to bubble.

02 Reduce to low and continue to cook, stirring occasionally, for 40 minutes – the rice should be *al dente* and not all of the liquid should have been absorbed.

TO COOK NOW: Leave the pan on the heat, stirring occasionally, until the rice is cooked through and the liquid is thickened and silky, around another 10 minutes. Serve hot.

TO FREEZE: Remove the pan from the heat and set aside to cool completely, then ladle the part-cooked mixture into a large, labelled freezer bag and freeze flat for up to 3 months.

TO COOK FROM FROZEN: Remove from the freezer and allow to completely defrost in the fridge. Once defrosted, transfer to a large pan and cook over a low heat for 8–10 minutes, stirring occasionally, until the rice is tender and the sauce is thick, velvety and piping hot. Serve.

To see a picture of this recipe, visit **thebatchlady.com/mealplanner**

Dairy	QTY		QTY
....	......	....	......
....	......	....	......
....	......	....	......
....	......	....	......
....	......	....	......

Storecupboard	QTY		QTY
....	......	....	......
....	......	....	......
....	......	....	......
....	......	....	......
....	......	....	......
....	......	....	......

Frozen Goods	QTY		QTY
....	......	....	......
....	......	....	......
....	......	....	......
....	......	....	......
....	......	....	......

Miscellaneous	QTY		QTY
....	......	....	......
....	......	....	......
....	......	....	......

Shopping list

Once you've planned what you are going to be cooking and eating during the week, use the template below to make a shopping list of the ingredients that you need to buy. If you're planning to batch any of the meals for later, remember to scale up the ingredients accordingly. Before buying anything, remember to check the storecupboard and freezer lists at the end of this book (pp.234–255) to check off any ingredients that you already have to hand at home.

Fruit & Vegetables	QTY		QTY
....	......	....	......
....	......	....	......
....	......	....	......
....	......	....	......
....	......	....	......
....	......	....	......
....	......	....	......

Meat & Fish	QTY		QTY
....	......	....	......
....	......	....	......
....	......	....	......
....	......	....	......
....	......	....	......
....	......	....	......

SATURDAY

Cooking

	DOUBLE UP	TO FREEZE
....	○	○
....	○	○
....	○	○
....	○	○

Eating

	FROZEN	FRESH
....	○	○
....	○	○
....	○	○
....	○	○

Doing

....

....

SUNDAY

Cooking

	DOUBLE UP	TO FREEZE
....	○	○
....	○	○
....	○	○
....	○	○

Eating

	FROZEN	FRESH
....	○	○
....	○	○
....	○	○
....	○	○

Doing

....

....

THURSDAY

Cooking

	TO FREEZE	DOUBLE UP
....	○	○
....	○	○
....	○	○
....	○	○

Eating

	FRESH	FROZEN
....	○	○
....	○	○
....	○	○
....	○	○

Doing

....

....

FRIDAY

Cooking

	TO FREEZE	DOUBLE UP
....	○	○
....	○	○
....	○	○
....	○	○

Eating

	FRESH	FROZEN
....	○	○
....	○	○
....	○	○
....	○	○

Doing

....

....

Cooking

DOUBLE UP
TO FREEZE

.... ◯ ◯

.... ◯ ◯

.... ◯ ◯

.... ◯ ◯

Eating

FROZEN
FRESH

.... ◯ ◯

.... ◯ ◯

.... ◯ ◯

.... ◯ ◯

Doing

....

....

Cooking

DOUBLE UP
TO FREEZE

.... ◯ ◯

.... ◯ ◯

.... ◯ ◯

.... ◯ ◯

Eating

FROZEN
FRESH

.... ◯ ◯

.... ◯ ◯

.... ◯ ◯

.... ◯ ◯

Doing

....

....

WEEK 22

Notes

MONDAY

Cooking

TO FREEZE · DOUBLE UP
○ ○
○ ○
○ ○
○ ○

Eating

FROZEN · FRESH
○ ○
○ ○
○ ○
○ ○

Doing

04 Unroll the pastry and cut each sheet into 8 equal squares, leaving you with 16 squares of pastry.

05 Divide the curried sweet potato mixture evenly between 8 of the pastry squares, then top each one with 1 teaspoon of the mango chutney.

05 Brush the edges of each filled square of pastry with some beaten egg, then top with one of the remaining squares of pastry and seal the edges by pressing with a fork. Using a sharp knife, cut a small hole in the top of each parcel to help steam escape as they cook.

TO COOK NOW: Place the parcels on a lined baking tray and brush the tops with more of the beaten egg. Transfer to an oven preheated to 180°C/350°F/gas mark 4 for 15 minutes, until the pastry is puffed and golden brown. Serve hot or cold.

....

TO FREEZE: Transfer the unbaked pockets to a large, labelled freezer bag and freeze flat for up to 3 months.

....

TO COOK FROM FROZEN:

These can be cooked straight from the freezer. Simply place the pockets on a lined baking tray and brush with a little beaten egg. Transfer to an oven preheated to 180°C/350°F/gas mark 4 for 20 minutes, until the pastry is puffed and golden brown. Serve hot or cold.

To see a picture of this recipe, visit
thebatchlady.com/mealplanner

CURRIED SWEET POTATO & PEA POCKETS

These spiced pastry pockets are wonderful eaten hot or cold and make a great veggie addition to a lunchbox or picnic.

PREP: 10 MINUTES
COOK: 20 MINUTES
MAKES 8

1½ cups (175g) frozen sweet potato chunks
1 cup (155g) frozen peas
1 tbsp vegetable oil
1 cup (115g) frozen chopped onions
1 tsp frozen chopped garlic
1 tbsp curry paste (I like to use korma)
juice of ½ lemon
2 sheets ready-rolled puff pastry
8 tsp mango chutney
1 egg, beaten

01 Bring a pan of water to the boil over a high heat, then add the sweet potato chunks, reduce the heat to a simmer and cook for 7 minutes. Add the peas to the pan and cook for 1 minute more, then drain the vegetables through a colander and set aside.

02 Heat the oil in a large frying pan over a medium heat, then add the onions and garlic and cook for 1 minute, stirring, until softened. Add the curry paste to the pan and cook for another minute, stirring, until fragrant.

03 Tip the cooked sweet potatoes and peas into the pan along with the lemon juice and give everything a stir to combine. Remove from the heat while you prepare the pastry.

Dairy   QTY   QTY

....
....
....
....
....

Storecupboard   QTY   QTY

....
....
....
....
....
....

Frozen Goods   QTY   QTY

....
....
....
....

Miscellaneous   QTY   QTY

....
....
....

Shopping list

Once you've planned what you are going to be cooking and eating during the week, use the template below to make a shopping list of the ingredients that you need to buy. If you're planning to batch any of the meals for later, remember to scale up the ingredients accordingly. Before buying anything, remember to check the storecupboard and freezer lists at the end of this book (pp.234–255) to check off any ingredients that you already have to hand at home.

Fruit & Vegetables	QTY		QTY
....	......	....	......
....	......	....	......
....	......	....	......
....	......	....	......
....	......	....	......
....	......	....	......
....	......	....	......

Meat & Fish	QTY		QTY
....	......	....	......
....	......	....	......
....	......	....	......
....	......	....	......
....	......	....	......

Cooking

DOUBLE UP
TO FREEZE

.... ○○
.... ○○
.... ○○
.... ○○

Eating

FROZEN
FRESH

.... ○○
.... ○○
.... ○○
.... ○○

Doing

....
....

Cooking

DOUBLE UP
TO FREEZE

.... ○○
.... ○○
.... ○○
.... ○○

Eating

FROZEN
FRESH

.... ○○
.... ○○
.... ○○
.... ○○

Doing

....
....

THURSDAY

Cooking

DOUBLE UP
TO FREEZE

.... ○○

.... ○○

.... ○○

.... ○○

Eating

FROZEN
FRESH

.... ○○

.... ○○

.... ○○

.... ○○

Doing

....

....

FRIDAY

Cooking

DOUBLE UP
TO FREEZE

.... ○○

.... ○○

.... ○○

.... ○○

Eating

FROZEN
FRESH

.... ○○

.... ○○

.... ○○

.... ○○

Doing

....

....

Cooking

TO FREEZE / DOUBLE UP

.... ○ ○
.... ○ ○
.... ○ ○
.... ○ ○

Eating

FROZEN / FRESH

.... ○ ○
.... ○ ○
.... ○ ○
.... ○ ○

Doing

....
....

WEDNESDAY

Cooking

TO FREEZE / DOUBLE UP

.... ○ ○
.... ○ ○
.... ○ ○
.... ○ ○

Eating

FROZEN / FRESH

.... ○ ○
.... ○ ○
.... ○ ○
.... ○ ○

Doing

....
....

WEEK 6

WEEK COMMENCING _____

Notes

....

....

....

....

MONDAY

Cooking	DOUBLE UP TO FREEZE
....	○ ○
....	○ ○
....	○ ○
....	○ ○

Eating	FROZEN FRESH
....	○ ○
....	○ ○
....	○ ○
....	○ ○

Doing

....

....

ORGANISE

your time so you can

ORGANISE

your mind

HONEY &
MUSTARD CHICKEN

This slow cooker recipe can be put on in the morning and left to simmer away. Come dinner time your house will smell delicious and you will have a dish to serve up that people will think you've slaved over.

PREP: 5 MINUTES
COOK: 6 HOURS
SERVES 4

4 skinless, boneless chicken
   breasts
1 tbsp wholegrain mustard
2 tbsp runny honey
1 tsp frozen chopped garlic
1 cup (115g) frozen chopped
   onions
1 cup (155g) frozen peas
1 cup (240ml) chicken stock
¼ cup (80g) crème fraîche
salt and freshly ground pepper
mashed potatoes and
   steamed green vegetables,
   to serve

01 If you are making this to serve the same day, put the chicken, mustard, honey, garlic, onions, peas, chicken stock and a grinding of salt and pepper into the pot of a slow cooker. If you are making this to freeze, put the same ingredients into a labelled freezer bag.

TO COOK NOW: Turn the slow cooker to low and leave to cook with the lid on for 5½ hours, then stir through the crème fraîche and continue to cook for another 30 minutes. Serve hot with mash and steamed green veg alongside.

TO FREEZE: Seal the freezer bag, squeezing out any excess air, transfer to the freezer and freeze flat for up to 3 months.

TO COOK FROM FROZEN: Remove from the freezer and allow to completely defrost in the fridge. Once defrosted, transfer to the slow cooker and cook as described in the *To Cook Now* section, above.

To see a picture of this recipe, visit
thebatchlady.com/mealplanner

Dairy　　　　　QTY　　　　　　　　　　　QTY

....　......　......................　......
....　......　......................　......
....　......　......................　......
....　......　......................　......
....　......　......................　......

Storecupboard　QTY　　　　　　　　　　　QTY

....　......　......................　......
....　......　......................　......
....　......　......................　......
....　......　......................　......
....　......　......................　......
....　......　......................　......

Frozen Goods　　QTY　　　　　　　　　　　QTY

....　......　......................　......
....　......　......................　......
....　......　......................　......
....　......　......................　......
....　......　......................　......

Miscellaneous　　QTY　　　　　　　　　　　QTY

....　......　......................　......
....　......　......................　......
....　......　......................　......

Shopping list

Once you've planned what you are going to be cooking and eating during the week, use the template below to make a shopping list of the ingredients that you need to buy. If you're planning to batch any of the meals for later, remember to scale up the ingredients accordingly. Before buying anything, remember to check the storecupboard and freezer lists at the end of this book (pp.234–255) to check off any ingredients that you already have to hand at home.

Fruit & Vegetables	QTY		QTY
....	......	....	......
....	......	....	......
....	......	....	......
....	......	....	......
....	......	....	......
....	......	....	......

Meat & Fish	QTY		QTY
....	......	....	......
....	......	....	......
....	......	....	......
....	......	....	......
....	......	....	......
....	......	....	......

Cooking

TO FREEZE
DOUBLE UP

.... ○ ○
.... ○ ○
.... ○ ○
.... ○ ○

Eating

FRESH
FROZEN

.... ○ ○
.... ○ ○
.... ○ ○
.... ○ ○

Doing

....
....

SUNDAY

Cooking

TO FREEZE
DOUBLE UP

.... ○ ○
.... ○ ○
.... ○ ○
.... ○ ○

Eating

FRESH
FROZEN

.... ○ ○
.... ○ ○
.... ○ ○
.... ○ ○

Doing

....
....

THURSDAY

Cooking | TO FREEZE | DOUBLE UP
.... ○ ○
.... ○ ○
.... ○ ○
.... ○ ○

Eating | FRESH | FROZEN
.... ○ ○
.... ○ ○
.... ○ ○
.... ○ ○

Doing
....
....

FRIDAY

Cooking | TO FREEZE | DOUBLE UP
.... ○ ○
.... ○ ○
.... ○ ○
.... ○ ○

Eating | FRESH | FROZEN
.... ○ ○
.... ○ ○
.... ○ ○
.... ○ ○

Doing
....
....

Cooking

	TO FREEZE	DOUBLE UP
....	○	○
....	○	○
....	○	○
....	○	○

Eating

	FRESH	FROZEN
....	○	○
....	○	○
....	○	○
....	○	○

Doing

....

....

Cooking

	TO FREEZE	DOUBLE UP
....	○	○
....	○	○
....	○	○
....	○	○

Eating

	FRESH	FROZEN
....	○	○
....	○	○
....	○	○
....	○	○

Doing

....

....

WEEK 5

Notes

....

....

....

....

MONDAY

Cooking

	DOUBLE UP TO FREEZE
....	○ ○
....	○ ○
....	○ ○
....	○ ○

Eating

	FROZEN FRESH
....	○ ○
....	○ ○
....	○ ○
....	○ ○

Doing

....

....

Batching

is not about

BEING PERFECT

it's about

HEADSPACE

FREEZER GUACAMOLE

Yes, you can freeze guacamole! The key is to freeze the basic mixture in portions (I use an ice cream scoop), then add any extras, such as tomato and red onion, at the last moment to give a really fresh and vibrant zing.

PREP: 10 MINUTES
SERVES 4–6

3 large, ripe avocados
splash of olive oil
juice of 2 limes
3 sprigs of coriander, leaves
 chopped
1 red chilli, deseeded and
 finely chopped
pinch of salt
2 large tomatoes, roughly
 chopped, to serve
½ red onion, finely chopped,
 to serve

01 Scoop the avocado flesh into a large bowl and add the olive oil, lime juice, chopped coriander leaves, chopped chilli and salt, then mash everything together to your preferred consistency with the back of a fork.

TO SERVE NOW: Stir through the chopped tomatoes and red onion and the guacamole is ready to serve. It makes a great dip for tortilla chips, is wonderful in fajitas or tacos or can be spread on toast and topped with a poached egg for an indulgent weekend breakfast.

TO FREEZE: Use an ice-cream scoop to portion the guacamole onto a lined baking tray. Place flat in the freezer for 1 hour, then transfer to a labelled freezer bag and freeze for up to 3 months.

TO SERVE FROM FROZEN: Remove as much of the guacamole as you need from the freezer and allow it to defrost in a bowl at room temperature – this should only take about an hour. Stir through some freshly chopped tomatoes and red onions and use the guacamole as described in the *To Serve Now* section, above.

To see a picture of this recipe, visit
thebatchlady.com/mealplanner

Dairy

	QTY		QTY
....	......	....	......
....	......	....	......
....	......	....	......
....	......	....	......

Storecupboard

	QTY		QTY
....	......	....	......
....	......	....	......
....	......	....	......
....	......	....	......

Frozen Goods

	QTY		QTY
....	......	....	......
....	......	....	......
....	......	....	......
....	......	....	......

Miscellaneous

	QTY		QTY
....	......	....	......
....	......	....	......
....	......	....	......

Shopping list

Once you've planned what you are going to be cooking and eating during the week, use the template below to make a shopping list of the ingredients that you need to buy. If you're planning to batch any of the meals for later, remember to scale up the ingredients accordingly. Before buying anything, remember to check the storecupboard and freezer lists at the end of this book (pp.234–255) to check off any ingredients that you already have to hand at home.

Fruit & Vegetables	QTY		QTY
....	......	....	......
....	......	....	......
....	......	....	......
....	......	....	......
....	......	....	......
....	......	....	......

Meat & Fish	QTY		QTY
....	......	....	......
....	......	....	......
....	......	....	......
....	......	....	......
....	......	....	......
....	......	....	......

SATURDAY

Cooking

DOUBLE UP
TO FREEZE

.... ○ ○

.... ○ ○

.... ○ ○

.... ○ ○

Eating

FROZEN
FRESH

.... ○ ○

.... ○ ○

.... ○ ○

.... ○ ○

Doing

....

....

SUNDAY

Cooking

DOUBLE UP
TO FREEZE

.... ○ ○

.... ○ ○

.... ○ ○

.... ○ ○

Eating

FROZEN
FRESH

.... ○ ○

.... ○ ○

.... ○ ○

.... ○ ○

Doing

....

....

THURSDAY

Cooking

	TO FREEZE	DOUBLE UP
....	○	○
....	○	○
....	○	○
....	○	○

Eating

	FRESH	FROZEN
....	○	○
....	○	○
....	○	○
....	○	○

Doing

....
....

FRIDAY

Cooking

	TO FREEZE	DOUBLE UP
....	○	○
....	○	○
....	○	○
....	○	○

Eating

	FRESH	FROZEN
....	○	○
....	○	○
....	○	○
....	○	○

Doing

....
....

TUESDAY

Cooking

	TO FREEZE	DOUBLE UP
....	○	○
....	○	○
....	○	○
....	○	○

Eating

	FRESH	FROZEN
....	○	○
....	○	○
....	○	○
....	○	○

Doing

....
....

WEDNESDAY

Cooking

	TO FREEZE	DOUBLE UP
....	○	○
....	○	○
....	○	○
....	○	○

Eating

	FRESH	FROZEN
....	○	○
....	○	○
....	○	○
....	○	○

Doing

....
....

WEEK 4

Notes

....

....

....

....

MONDAY

Cooking

	TO FREEZE	DOUBLE UP
....	○	○
....	○	○
....	○	○
....	○	○

Eating

	FRESH	FROZEN
....	○	○
....	○	○
....	○	○
....	○	○

Doing

....

....

05 Pour the mixture into the prepared loaf tin and level out with a spoon.

06 Transfer to the oven and bake for 30–40 minutes until golden, well risen and a skewer inserted into the centre of the loaf comes out clean. Set aside to cool.

TO SERVE NOW: Once cooled, turn the cake out of the tin, cut into slices and serve.

....

TO FREEZE: Once cooled, turn the cake out of the tin, cut into slices and wrap each in a layer of clingfilm followed by a layer of foil. Store the slices flat in the freezer for up to 3 months.

....

TO SERVE FROM FROZEN: Remove individual slices of the cake from the freezer as needed and set on the counter to defrost. They should be ready to eat in around 30 minutes.

Zhuzh it up!
To make this extra special, serve the slices with a sprinkling of cinnamon sugar and a scoop of vanilla ice ceam (p.216) on the side.

To see a picture of this recipe, visit
thebatchlady.com/mealplanner

BANANA & CINNAMON BREAD

This is the perfect recipe for the times when you have bananas that are past their best sitting in the fruit bowl. It makes a wonderful treat breakfast or afternoon snack and individual slices can be stored in the freezer and quickly defrosted when guests pop by unnanounced.

PREP: 8–10 MINUTES
COOK: 30–40 MINUTES
MAKES 1 x 900G (2LB) LOAF CAKE

¾ cup (180g) unsalted butter, at room temperature
1 cup (200g) caster sugar
2 eggs, beaten
1½ cups (200g) self-raising flour
1 tsp baking powder
½ tsp ground cinnamon
2 tbsp whole or semi-skimmed milk
2 ripe bananas

01 Preheat the oven to 180°C/350°F/gas mark 4. Grease a 900g (2lb) loaf tin with butter and line with greaseproof paper.

02 In a large bowl, beat the butter and sugar together with an electric whisk until light and airy. Add the eggs and beat again until well combined.

03 Sift in the flour, baking powder and ground cinnamon and mix again until just combined, then add the milk and mix again briefly.

04 In a separate bowl, mash the bananas with a fork, then add to the rest of the ingredients and gently fold into the mixture with a wooden spoon.

Dairy	QTY		QTY

Storecupboard	QTY		QTY

Frozen Goods	QTY		QTY

Miscellaneous	QTY		QTY

Shopping list

Once you've planned what you are going to be cooking and eating during the week, use the template below to make a shopping list of the ingredients that you need to buy. If you're planning to batch any of the meals for later, remember to scale up the ingredients accordingly. Before buying anything, remember to check the storecupboard and freezer lists at the end of this book (pp.234–255) to check off any ingredients that you already have to hand at home.

Fruit & Vegetables	QTY		QTY

Meat & Fish	QTY		QTY

Cooking

	TO FREEZE	DOUBLE UP
....	○	○
....	○	○
....	○	○
....	○	○

Eating

	FROZEN	FRESH
....	○	○
....	○	○
....	○	○
....	○	○

Doing

....

....

Cooking

	TO FREEZE	DOUBLE UP
....	○	○
....	○	○
....	○	○
....	○	○

Eating

	FROZEN	FRESH
....	○	○
....	○	○
....	○	○
....	○	○

Doing

....

....

THURSDAY

Cooking

DOUBLE UP
TO FREEZE

.... ◯ ◯

.... ◯ ◯

.... ◯ ◯

.... ◯ ◯

Eating

FROZEN
FRESH

.... ◯ ◯

.... ◯ ◯

.... ◯ ◯

.... ◯ ◯

Doing

....

....

FRIDAY

Cooking

DOUBLE UP
TO FREEZE

.... ◯ ◯

.... ◯ ◯

.... ◯ ◯

.... ◯ ◯

Eating

FROZEN
FRESH

.... ◯ ◯

.... ◯ ◯

.... ◯ ◯

.... ◯ ◯

Doing

....

....

TUESDAY

Cooking

DOUBLE UP
TO FREEZE

.... ⭘⭘

.... ⭘⭘

.... ⭘⭘

.... ⭘⭘

Eating

FROZEN
FRESH

.... ⭘⭘

.... ⭘⭘

.... ⭘⭘

.... ⭘⭘

Doing

....

....

WEDNESDAY

Cooking

DOUBLE UP
TO FREEZE

.... ⭘⭘

.... ⭘⭘

.... ⭘⭘

.... ⭘⭘

Eating

FROZEN
FRESH

.... ⭘⭘

.... ⭘⭘

.... ⭘⭘

.... ⭘⭘

Doing

....

....

WEEK 3

Notes

....

....

....

....

MONDAY

Cooking

DOUBLE UP TO FREEZE

.... ○ ○

.... ○ ○

.... ○ ○

.... ○ ○

Eating

FROZEN FRESH

.... ○ ○

.... ○ ○

.... ○ ○

.... ○ ○

Doing

....

....

Lighten
* * * * * *
YOUR MENTAL
LOAD BY

Planning
IN ADVANCE

RED PESTO

This fiery pesto can be whipped up in seconds, frozen in cubes and whipped out of the freezer at a moment's notice to add a burst of flavour to any meal. It is wonderful on pasta, served with grilled fish or meats, or even smeared on a toastie before grilling.

PREP: 5 MINUTES
MAKES 1 CUP (240ML)

1 large jar (270g drained
  weight) semi-dried
  tomatoes in oil, drained
¼ cup (35g) pine nuts
2 tsp frozen chopped red
  chillies
1 tsp frozen chopped garlic
½ tsp salt
handful of flat-leaf parsley
½ cup (120ml) olive oil (you
  can use the oil from the
  semi-dried tomato jar)

01 Transfer all of the ingredients to a blender and blend to your desired consistency, depending whether you prefer a coarser or smoother pesto. If the mixture is too dry, simply drizzle in a little more oil.

TO USE NOW: The pesto is now ready to use. It is delicious used to dress pasta or spooned over grilled fish or meats.

....

TO FREEZE: I like to freeze pesto in ice cube trays so that I can defrost as much or as little as I want at any one time. Simply spoon the mixture into ice cube trays and freeze flat for a couple of hours, then pop out the cubes, transfer to a labelled freezer bag and return to the freezer for up to 3 months.

....

TO COOK FROM FROZEN:
The cubes of pesto will defrost really quickly when added to a hot pan, simply add as many as you need and cook, stirring until defrosted, then use as described in the *To Use Now* section, above.

To see a picture of this recipe, visit
thebatchlady.com/mealplanner

Dairy

	QTY		QTY
....	......	....	......
....	......	....	......
....	......	....	......
....	......	....	......
....	......	....	......

Storecupboard

	QTY		QTY
....	......	....	......
....	......	....	......
....	......	....	......
....	......	....	......
....	......	....	......

Frozen Goods

	QTY		QTY
....	......	....	......
....	......	....	......
....	......	....	......
....	......	....	......
....	......	....	......

Miscellaneous

	QTY		QTY
....	......	....	......
....	......	....	......
....	......	....	......

Shopping list

Once you've planned what you are going to be cooking and eating during the week, use the template below to make a shopping list of the ingredients that you need to buy. If you're planning to batch any of the meals for later, remember to scale up the ingredients accordingly. Before buying anything, remember to check the storecupboard and freezer lists at the end of this book (pp.234–255) to check off any ingredients that you already have to hand at home.

Fruit & Vegetables	QTY		QTY
....	.....	....	.....
....	.....	....	.....
....	.....	....	.....
....	.....	....	.....
....	.....	....	.....

Meat & Fish	QTY		QTY
....	.....	....	.....
....	.....	....	.....
....	.....	....	.....
....	.....	....	.....
....	.....	....	.....

SATURDAY

Cooking

	TO FREEZE	DOUBLE UP
....	◯	◯
....	◯	◯
....	◯	◯
....	◯	◯

Eating

	FRESH	FROZEN
....	◯	◯
....	◯	◯
....	◯	◯
....	◯	◯

Doing

....
....

SUNDAY

Cooking

	TO FREEZE	DOUBLE UP
....	◯	◯
....	◯	◯
....	◯	◯
....	◯	◯

Eating

	FRESH	FROZEN
....	◯	◯
....	◯	◯
....	◯	◯
....	◯	◯

Doing

....
....

THURSDAY

Cooking

TO FREEZE · DOUBLE UP

.... ○ ○

.... ○ ○

.... ○ ○

.... ○ ○

Eating

FRESH · FROZEN

.... ○ ○

.... ○ ○

.... ○ ○

.... ○ ○

Doing

....

....

FRIDAY

Cooking

TO FREEZE · DOUBLE UP

.... ○ ○

.... ○ ○

.... ○ ○

.... ○ ○

Eating

FRESH · FROZEN

.... ○ ○

.... ○ ○

.... ○ ○

.... ○ ○

Doing

....

....

TUESDAY

Cooking

	TO FREEZE	DOUBLE UP
....	○	○
....	○	○
....	○	○
....	○	○

Eating

	FRESH	FROZEN
....	○	○
....	○	○
....	○	○
....	○	○

Doing

....
....

WEDNESDAY

Cooking

	TO FREEZE	DOUBLE UP
....	○	○
....	○	○
....	○	○
....	○	○

Eating

	FRESH	FROZEN
....	○	○
....	○	○
....	○	○
....	○	○

Doing

....
....

WEEK 2

Notes

....

....

....

....

MONDAY

Cooking	TO FREEZE	DOUBLE UP
....	○	○
....	○	○
....	○	○
....	○	○

Eating	FRESH	FROZEN
....	○	○
....	○	○
....	○	○
....	○	○

Doing

....

....

THE FIRST *Step* IS ALWAYS THE *hardest*

GREEN PESTO

Making pesto is so simple to do but somehow makes me feel like a domestic goddess! Both this and the Red Pesto recipe (p.34) use similar ingredients, so why not knock up both batches at once?

PREP: 5 MINUTES
MAKES ABOUT 1 CUP (240ML)

2 cups (about 60g) basil leaves
5 tbsp pine nuts
5 tbsp pre-grated Parmesan cheese
2 tsp frozen chopped garlic
½ tsp salt
⅔ cup (160ml) olive oil

01 Simply transfer all of the ingredients to a blender and blend to your desired consistency, depending whether you prefer a coarser or smoother pesto. If the mixture is too dry, simply add a little more oil.

TO USE NOW: The pesto is now ready to use. It is delicious used to dress pasta or spooned over grilled fish or meats.

....

TO FREEZE: I like to freeze pesto in ice cube trays so that I can defrost as much or as little as I want at any one time. Simply spoon the mixture into ice cube trays and freeze flat for a couple of hours, then pop out the cubes, transfer to a labelled freezer bag and return to the freezer for up to 3 months.

....

TO COOK FROM FROZEN: The cubes of pesto will defrost really quickly when added to a hot pan, simply add as many as you need and cook, stirring until defrosted, then use as described in the *To Use Now* section, above.

To see a picture of this recipe, visit
thebatchlady.com/mealplanner

Dairy	QTY		QTY
....	......	....	......
....	......	....	......
....	......	....	......
....	......	....	......
....	......	....	......

Storecupboard	QTY		QTY
....	......	....	......
....	......	....	......
....	......	....	......
....	......	....	......
....	......	....	......

Frozen Goods	QTY		QTY
....	......	....	......
....	......	....	......
....	......	....	......
....	......	....	......
....	......	....	......

Miscellaneous	QTY		QTY
....	......	....	......
....	......	....	......
....	......	....	......

Shopping list

Once you've planned what you are going to be cooking and eating during the week, use the template below to make a shopping list of the ingredients that you need to buy. If you're planning to batch any of the meals for later, remember to scale up the ingredients accordingly. Before buying anything, remember to check the storecupboard and freezer lists at the end of this book (pp.234–255) to check off any ingredients that you already have to hand at home.

Fruit & Vegetables	QTY		QTY

Meat & Fish	QTY		QTY

Cooking

TO FREEZE · DOUBLE UP

.... ○ ○

.... ○ ○

.... ○ ○

.... ○ ○

Eating

FRESH · FROZEN

.... ○ ○

.... ○ ○

.... ○ ○

.... ○ ○

Doing

....

....

SUNDAY

Cooking

TO FREEZE · DOUBLE UP

.... ○ ○

.... ○ ○

.... ○ ○

.... ○ ○

Eating

FRESH · FROZEN

.... ○ ○

.... ○ ○

.... ○ ○

.... ○ ○

Doing

....

....

THURSDAY

Cooking

TO FREEZE DOUBLE UP

.... ○ ○
.... ○ ○
.... ○ ○
.... ○ ○

Eating

FRESH FROZEN

.... ○ ○
.... ○ ○
.... ○ ○
.... ○ ○

Doing

....
....

FRIDAY

Cooking

TO FREEZE DOUBLE UP

.... ○ ○
.... ○ ○
.... ○ ○
.... ○ ○

Eating

FRESH FROZEN

.... ○ ○
.... ○ ○
.... ○ ○
.... ○ ○

Doing

....
....

Cooking
DOUBLE UP
TO FREEZE

.... ○ ○
.... ○ ○
.... ○ ○
.... ○ ○

Eating
FROZEN
FRESH

.... ○ ○
.... ○ ○
.... ○ ○
.... ○ ○

Doing

....

....

WEDNESDAY

Cooking
DOUBLE UP
TO FREEZE

.... ○ ○
.... ○ ○
.... ○ ○
.... ○ ○

Eating
FROZEN
FRESH

.... ○ ○
.... ○ ○
.... ○ ○
.... ○ ○

Doing

....

....

WEEK 1

Notes

....

....

....

....

MONDAY

Cooking

	TO FREEZE	DOUBLE UP
....	○	○
....	○	○
....	○	○
....	○	○

Eating

	FRESH	FROZEN
....	○	○
....	○	○
....	○	○
....	○	○

Doing

....

....

YOUR

WEEKLY
· · · · · · · · · ·
PLANNERS

Shopping list

Once you've planned what you are going to be cooking and eating during the week, use the template below to make a shopping list of the ingredients that you need to buy. If you're planning to batch any of the meals for later, remember to scale up the ingredients accordingly. Before buying anything, remember to check the storecupboard and freezer lists at the end of this book (pp.234–255) to check off any ingredients that you already have to hand at home.

Fruit & Vegetables	QTY		QTY
....	......	....	......
....	......	....	......
....	......	....	......
....	......	....	......
....	......	....	......
....	......	....	......

Meat & Fish	QTY		QTY
....	......	....	......
....	......	....	......
....	......	....	......
....	......	....	......
....	......	....	......
....	......	....	......

SATURDAY

Cooking
TO FREEZE / DOUBLE UP

.... ○ ○

.... ○ ○

.... ○ ○

.... ○ ○

Eating
FRESH / FROZEN

.... ○ ○

.... ○ ○

.... ○ ○

.... ○ ○

Doing

....

....

SUNDAY

Cooking
TO FREEZE / DOUBLE UP

.... ○ ○

.... ○ ○

.... ○ ○

.... ○ ○

Eating
FRESH / FROZEN

.... ○ ○

.... ○ ○

.... ○ ○

.... ○ ○

Doing

....

....

THURSDAY

Cooking

DOUBLE UP
TO FREEZE

.... ○ ○

.... ○ ○

.... ○ ○

.... ○ ○

Eating

FROZEN
FRESH

.... ○ ○

.... ○ ○

.... ○ ○

.... ○ ○

Doing

....

....

FRIDAY

Cooking

DOUBLE UP
TO FREEZE

.... ○ ○

.... ○ ○

.... ○ ○

.... ○ ○

Eating

FROZEN
FRESH

.... ○ ○

.... ○ ○

.... ○ ○

.... ○ ○

Doing

....

....

TUESDAY

Cooking

	TO FREEZE	DOUBLE UP
....	○	○
....	○	○
....	○	○
....	○	○

Eating

	FRESH	FROZEN
....	○	○
....	○	○
....	○	○
....	○	○

Doing

....

....

WEDNESDAY

Cooking

	TO FREEZE	DOUBLE UP
....	○	○
....	○	○
....	○	○
....	○	○

Eating

	FRESH	FROZEN
....	○	○
....	○	○
....	○	○
....	○	○

Doing

....

....

WEEK 18

Notes

....

....

....

....

MONDAY

Cooking

DOUBLE UP
TO FREEZE

.... ○ ○

.... ○ ○

.... ○ ○

.... ○ ○

Eating

FROZEN
FRESH

.... ○ ○

.... ○ ○

.... ○ ○

.... ○ ○

Doing

....

....

TO COOK NOW: Continue to cook, stirring occasionally, for another 5 minutes, until the pasta is tender and most of the liquid has been absorbed. Remove from the heat, stir in the Parmesan and crème fraîche and season to taste. Serve hot.

....

TO FREEZE: Remove from the heat, stir in the Parmesan and crème fraîche and season to taste. Set the pan aside until the orzo has completely cooled, then ladle the part-cooked mixture into a large, labelled freezer bag and freeze flat for up to 3 months.

....

TO COOK FROM FROZEN: Remove from the freezer and allow to completely defrost in the fridge. Once defrosted, tip the orzo mixture into a large pan with 2–3 tablespoons of chicken stock and cook for 5–10 minutes, stirring, until the pasta is tender and piping hot. Serve.

Zhuzh it up!
Sprinkle the finished dish with some dried chilli flakes for a fiery hit. This works well when serving the dish to a mixed group as everyone can make it as spicy as they like!

To see a picture of this recipe, visit
thebatchlady.com/mealplanner

BACON & MUSHROOM ORZO

Comfort food at its best, orzo works really well in this delicious brothy bowl laden with tasty bacon and mushrooms.

PREP: 5 MINUTES
COOK: 12 MINUTES
SERVES 4

1 tbsp olive oil
1 cup (115g) frozen chopped onions
200g bacon lardons (smoked or unsmoked)
500g white mushrooms, sliced
1 tsp frozen chopped garlic
3 cups (720ml) chicken stock, plus an extra 2–3 tbsp if cooking from frozen
2 cups (400g) orzo
1 cup (70g) pre-grated Parmesan cheese
½ cup (120ml) crème fraîche
salt and freshly ground pepper

01 Heat the oil in a large sauté pan over a medium heat, then add the onions, bacon lardons, mushrooms and garlic. Fry the mixture, stirring, until all the elements are crisp and golden, around 10 minutes.

02 Add the chicken stock and orzo to the pan and stir to combine. Bring the mixture to a simmer, then leave to cook, stirring occasionally, for 7 minutes. At this point the pasta should still be slightly firm and won't have absorbed all of the liquid.

Dairy QTY QTY

....
....
....
....
....

Storecupboard QTY QTY

....
....
....
....
....
....

Frozen Goods QTY QTY

....
....
....
....
....

Miscellaneous QTY QTY

....
....
....

Cooking

DOUBLE UP
TO FREEZE

.... ○○

.... ○○

.... ○○

.... ○○

Eating

FROZEN
FRESH

.... ○○

.... ○○

.... ○○

.... ○○

Doing

....

....

Cooking

DOUBLE UP
TO FREEZE

.... ○○

.... ○○

.... ○○

.... ○○

Eating

FROZEN
FRESH

.... ○○

.... ○○

.... ○○

.... ○○

Doing

....

....

Shopping list

Once you've planned what you are going to be cooking and eating during the week, use the template below to make a shopping list of the ingredients that you need to buy. If you're planning to batch any of the meals for later, remember to scale up the ingredients accordingly. Before buying anything, remember to check the storecupboard and freezer lists at the end of this book (pp.234–255) to check off any ingredients that you already have to hand at home.

Fruit & Vegetables	QTY		QTY
....	......	....	......
....	......	....	......
....	......	....	......
....	......	....	......
....	......	....	......
....	......	....	......

Meat & Fish	QTY		QTY
....	......	....	......
....	......	....	......
....	......	....	......
....	......	....	......
....	......	....	......

Dairy	QTY	Storecupboard	QTY
....	......	....	......
....	......	....	......
....	......	....	......
....	......	....	......

Storecupboard	QTY	Frozen Goods	QTY
....	......	....	......
....	......	....	......
....	......	....	......
....	......	....	......

Frozen Goods	QTY	Miscellaneous	QTY
....	......	....	......
....	......	....	......
....	......	....	......
....	......	....	......

Miscellaneous	QTY		QTY
....	......	....	......
....	......	....	......
....	......	....	......

VANILLA ICE CREAM

Many people wouldn't even consider making ice cream at home, but this super quick version is as good as any variety that you can buy in the shops and much kinder on the wallet! If you like, you can ripple through some raspberry coulis, chocolate chips or Biscoff spread at the end of step 1 for an extra indulgent treat.

PREP: 5 MINUTES, PLUS FREEZING

SERVES 4

1 x 600ml pot double cream
1 x 397g can sweetened condensed milk
1 tsp vanilla extract

TO SERVE FROM FROZEN:
Once set, the ice cream can be served immediately.

01 Put the double cream, condensed milk and vanilla extract in a large bowl and stir gently to just combine, then, using an electric whisk, whisk the mixture until thick, about 5 minutes.

02 Transfer the mixture to a freezer proof dish and cover with a lid or a layer of clingfilm followed by a layer of foil. Transfer to the freezer until completely set.

To see a picture of this recipe, visit
thebatchlady.com/mealplanner

EAT WELL
ALL WEEK

EAT WELL

COOK
ONCE

SHOP
ONCE

Batch Day

DATE

Use this page to plan for the days when you want to tackle a dedicated batching session, making several meals at once to fill your freezer. Write a list of the meals that you want to make below, making sure to mark if you're planning to double up any of the recipes. Once you've planned what you're going to cook, use the shopping list opposite to write down what you need to buy.

I like to do a special visit to the shops or order online when planning a batch day, as that way I can lay everything out on the sides when I get home and am ready to start, without having to scrabble around in the cupboards trying to find things while I'm cooking.

What I'm cooking

Double Up

○ ....
○ ....
○ ....
○ ....
○ ....
○ ....
○ ....
○ ....
○ ....

Notes

....
....
....
....

BATCH DAY SHOPPING LIST

Fruit & Vegetables	QTY		QTY
....	......	....	......
....	......	....	......
....	......	....	......
Meat & Fish	QTY		QTY
....	......	....	......
....	......	....	......
....	......	....	......
Dairy	QTY		QTY
....	......	....	......
....	......	....	......
....	......	....	......
Storecupboard	QTY		QTY
....	......	....	......
....	......	....	......
....	......	....	......
Frozen Goods	QTY		QTY
....	......	....	......
....	......	....	......
....	......	....	......

WEEK 25

WEEK COMMENCING ----------------

Notes
....
....
....
....

MONDAY

Eating
FROZEN FRESH
○○ ....
○○ ....
○○ ....
○○ ....

Cooking
DOUBLE UP TO FREEZE
○○ ....
○○ ....
○○ ....
○○ ....

Doug
....
....

TUESDAY

Eating

FROZEN
FRESH
○○ ....
○○ ....
○○ ....
○○ ....

Cooking

DOUBLE UP
TO FREEZE
○○ ....
○○ ....
○○ ....
○○ ....

Doug
....
....

WEDNESDAY

Eating

FROZEN
FRESH
○○ ....
○○ ....
○○ ....
○○ ....

Cooking

DOUBLE UP
TO FREEZE
○○ ....
○○ ....
○○ ....
○○ ....

Doug
....
....

THURSDAY

Eating
FROZEN FRESH
OO ....
OO ....
OO ....
OO ....

Cooking
DOUBLE UP TO FREEZE
OO ....
OO ....
OO ....
OO ....

Doing
....
....

FRIDAY

Eating
FROZEN FRESH
OO ....
OO ....
OO ....
OO ....

Cooking
DOUBLE UP TO FREEZE
OO ....
OO ....
OO ....
OO ....

Doing
....
....

SATURDAY

Cooking

DOUBLE UP ○
TO FREEZE ○ ·······························
○ ○ ·······························
○ ○ ·······························
○ ○ ·······························

Eating

FROZEN ○
FRESH ○ ·······························
○ ○ ·······························
○ ○ ·······························
○ ○ ·······························

Doing

··

··

SUNDAY

Cooking

DOUBLE UP ○
TO FREEZE ○ ·······························
○ ○ ·······························
○ ○ ·······························
○ ○ ·······························

Eating

FROZEN ○
FRESH ○ ·······························
○ ○ ·······························
○ ○ ·······························
○ ○ ·······························

Doing

··

··

Shopping list

Once you've planned what you are going to be cooking and eating during the week, use the template below to make a shopping list of the ingredients that you need to buy. If you're planning to batch any of the meals for later, remember to scale up the ingredients accordingly. Before buying anything, remember to check the storecupboard and freezer lists at the end of this book (pp.234–255) to check off any ingredients that you already have to hand at home.

Fruit & Vegetables	QTY		QTY

Meat & Fish	QTY		QTY

	QTY		QTY
Dairy			
Storecupboard			QTY
Frozen Goods			QTY
Miscellaneous			QTY

CHEESY BACON & ONION POCKETS

These delicious pastry pockets are stuffed with bacon, cheese and onions and can be eaten hot or cold, making them a wonderfully filling option for a lunchbox or picnic.

PREP: 10 MINUTES
COOK: 15-20 MINUTES
MAKES 8

2 Maris Piper potatoes, peeled and cut into 1cm (½in) cubes
1 tbsp vegetable oil
knob of butter
200g bacon lardons
1 cup (115g) frozen chopped onions
2 sheets ready-rolled puff pastry
8 tbsp pre-grated Cheddar cheese
1 egg, beaten

01 Bring a pan of water to the boil over a high heat, add the potatoes and reduce the heat to a simmer. Cook for 6 minutes, until just tender. Drain through a colander and set aside to steam dry.

02 Heat the oil and butter in a large saucepan over a medium heat, then add the bacon lardons, onions and cooked potato. Fry the mixture, stirring regularly, until all the elements are crisp and golden, around 10 minutes. Remove from the heat while you prepare the pastry.

03 Unroll the pastry and cut each sheet into 8 equal squares, leaving you with 16 squares of pastry.

04 Divide the potato and bacon mixture evenly between 8 of the pastry squares, then top each one with 1 tablespoon of Cheddar cheese.

05 Brush the edges of each filled square of pastry with some beaten egg, then top with one of the remaining squares of pastry and seal the edges by pressing with a fork. Using a sharp knife, cut a small hole in the top of each parcel to help steam escape as they cook.

TO COOK NOW: Place the parcels on a lined baking tray and brush the tops with more of the beaten egg. Transfer to an oven preheated to 180°C/350°F/gas mark 4 for 18 minutes, until the pastry is puffed and golden brown. Serve hot or cold.

TO FREEZE: Transfer the unbaked pockets to a large, labelled freezer bag and freeze flat for up to 3 months.

TO COOK FROM FROZEN:
These can be cooked straight from the freezer. Simply place the pockets on a lined baking tray and brush with a little beaten egg. Transfer to an oven preheated to 180°C/350°F/gas mark 4 for 20–25 minutes, until the pastry is puffed and golden brown. Serve hot or cold.

To see a picture of this recipe, visit
thebatchlady.com/mealplanner

Doing

....
....

MONDAY

Eating

FROZEN
FRESH

OO ....
OO ....
OO ....
OO ....

Cooking

DOUBLE UP
TO FREEZE

OO ....
OO ....
OO ....
OO ....

Notes

....
....
....
....

WEEK 26

WEDNESDAY

Eating

FROZEN FRESH

Cooking

DOUBLE UP TO FREEZE

Doing

TUESDAY

Eating

FROZEN FRESH

Cooking

DOUBLE UP TO FREEZE

Doing

THURSDAY

Eating

FROZEN FRESH
.... ⭕⭕
.... ⭕⭕
.... ⭕⭕
.... ⭕⭕

Cooking

DOUBLE UP TO FREEZE
.... ⭕⭕
.... ⭕⭕
.... ⭕⭕
.... ⭕⭕

Doing
....
....

FRIDAY

Eating

FROZEN FRESH
.... ⭕⭕
.... ⭕⭕
.... ⭕⭕
.... ⭕⭕

Cooking

DOUBLE UP TO FREEZE
.... ⭕⭕
.... ⭕⭕
.... ⭕⭕
.... ⭕⭕

Doing
....
....

SUNDAY

Eating

FROZEN FRESH

Cooking

DOUBLE UP TO FREEZE

Doug

SATURDAY

Eating

FROZEN FRESH

Cooking

DOUBLE UP TO FREEZE

Doug

Shopping list

Once you've planned what you are going to be cooking and eating during the week, use the template below to make a shopping list of the ingredients that you need to buy. If you're planning to batch any of the meals for later, remember to scale up the ingredients accordingly. Before buying anything, remember to check the storecupboard and freezer lists at the end of this book (pp.234–255) to check off any ingredients that you already have to hand at home.

Fruit & Vegetables	QTY		QTY
....	.....	....	.....
....	.....	....	.....
....	.....	....	.....
....	.....	....	.....
....	.....	....	.....
....	.....	....	.....

Meat & Fish	QTY		QTY
....	.....	....	.....
....	.....	....	.....
....	.....	....	.....
....	.....	....	.....
....	.....	....	.....
....	.....	....	.....